Earth Changes
UPDATE

Earth Changes

UPDATE

by Hugh Lynn Cayce

Including the complete text of
Earth Changes: Past—Present—Future
by a Geologist

ARE
PRESS

ASSOCIATION FOR
RESEARCH AND
ENLIGHTENMENT

A.R.E. PRESS • VIRGINIA BEACH • VIRGINIA

Part II, "Earth Changes: Past—Present—Future,"
was originally published in January, 1959, under the
title, "A Psychic Interpretation of Some Late-Cenozoic
Events Compared with Selected Scientific Data." It was
revised and augmented in 1961, 1963 and 1968.
"Atlantis at Bimini" was published in *The A.R.E.
Journal*, Volume III, Number 3, copyright 1968 by the
Association for Research and Enlightenment, Inc.

ISBN 87604-121-7

14th Printing, May 1997

Cover design by Richard Boyle

CONTENTS

CONTENTS

Foreword

Edgar Cayce predicted in his psychic discourses, called "readings," that the earth would be greatly changed during the years 1958 to 1998. We have passed the midpoint of that forty-year period, and changes are now being felt. The frequency of earthquakes seems to be increasing; weather patterns seem to be shifting. Attitudes are changing; new spiritual awarenesses are being born.

At the beginning of this period the A.R.E. published a booklet entitled *Earth Changes: Past—Present—Future*. The booklet was enlarged somewhat through the '60s but eventually went out of print in 1971 at the request of the author (a geologist who wishes to remain anonymous) because he felt that the book was becoming dated. The demand for the booklet, though, has remained high.

As the first half of the 1958-1998 period was completed, it became obvious that many people were increasingly interested in the subject of earth changes. We decided that an update was called for. The original *Earth Changes* booklet has been reprinted (as Part II) both for historical perspective and for the large amount of information it presents. In Part I Hugh Lynn Cayce examines the many instances of current events which corroborate his father's readings. He also discusses the problems involved in working with psychic material. And finally he suggests the emphasis needed to prepare for the coming changes.

The readings from which the predictions come are dated to give the reader the proper chronology of the predictions. The reading number identifies the person or group for whom the reading was given. For example, reading 294-31 was the 31st reading given for the person numbered 294. It should also be noted that the earth changes prophecies for the most part were given incidentally in general readings or in answer to specific questions. Only a few readings were given with predictions of these events as the main focus.

The accuracy of the Cayce material has been demonstrated over the years by personal testimony after a medical problem was diagnosed and by observation when world events or prophecy was involved. The high correlation between predictions and events prompted Jess Stearn to write his best seller, *Edgar Cayce, the Sleeping Prophet,* in 1967.

We hope that this update will further aid readers in observing and assessing the events which mark the beginning of a new age.

The Editors

Part I
Earth Changes Update
by Hugh Lynn Cayce

Chapter I

PREDICTIONS AND THE PRESS

Edgar Cayce throughout his lifetime welcomed and encouraged people to check the accuracy of the information that came through him. The physical readings with their medical diagnoses and suggestions were available for immediate checking. The mental-spiritual readings could be attested at a personal level. The life readings, also, could be personally evidential. But the predictions and prophecies in the readings have had to wait for the years to pass and time to prove or disprove them. Some of these have already been verified. Some wait.

Gladys Davis Turner, Edgar Cayce's lifelong secretary, has maintained a file of clippings which pertain to information in the readings, often appending them to the transcripts of the readings in the A.R.E. Library. Throughout the years members of the Association have sent applicable news items to the A.R.E. Headquarters, and no subject has been of greater general interest than Earth Changes. We present here selections from these files which verify specific earth changes predictions. Sometimes we have used only headlines to tell the story. At other times we've reproduced several paragraphs, or the article in its entirety.

The words below were uttered almost as an afterthought, in a reading given by Edgar Cayce on August 27, 1926. As is indicated in another section of this book (see pp. 79-80), these statements in the readings, made approximately two months prior to the activities described, were confirmed by later weather reports. Several points of confirmation were included—all close to or on the dates indicated: violent wind storms, north Atlantic; Cuba, worst storm on record; hurricane in vicinity of Kuril Island (near Japan); California and Japan quakes, one on October 22, the other on the 19th and 20th of October; however, no severe tidal waves were reported.

. . .As has been oft given, Jupiter and Uranus influences in the affairs of the world appear the strongest on or about October 15 to 20th when there may be expected in the minds, the actions—not only of individuals, but in various quarters of the globe—destructive conditions as well as building. In the affairs of man many conditions will arise that will be very, very strange to the world at present—in religion, in politics, in the moral conditions, and in the attempt to curb or to change such, see? For there will be set in motion [that indicating] when prohibition will be lost in America, see? *Violent wind storms—two earthquakes, one occurring in California, another in Japan*—tidal waves following, one to the southern portion of the isles near Japan! [Author's italics]   195-32

"South America shall be shaken. . ."

Another reading contained predictions in reference to South America:

South America shall be shaken from the uppermost portion to the end, and in the Antarctic off of Tierra Del Fuego *land*, and a strait with rushing waters.   3976-15, Jan. 19, 1934

Edgar Cayce's statement, "South America shall be shaken from the uppermost portion to the end. . ." has become grim historical fact, which continues to unfold in our time.   On June 1, 1970, *The Los Angeles Herald Examiner* reported with a Lima, Peru, dateline:

TREMORS JAR HALF OF NATION

A *New York Times* headline on June 2, 1970, read:

30,000 FEARED DEAD IN PERU QUAKE

The article reported "incredible property damage—thousands of buildings destroyed"; "The cities of Huaras and Caras were reported 90% destroyed." By June 9, 1970, the deaths topped 50,000.

In a July 9, 1970, article in *The New York Times* titled "Evidence of Moving Earth Plates Is Found," we learn that oceanographers from the Navy and from Princeton University discovered that three great plates of the earth's surface are being pushed apart southwest of Central America. They said that such motion could account for the severe Peruvian earthquake of June 1.

On October 4, 1974, the *El Paso Herald-Post* reported:

70,000 HOMELESS FROM PERU QUAKE

A portion of this article has been excerpted:

"Authorities said today dozens of persons died and thousands were injured by an earthquake that jolted Peru's central coast, pushed back Pacific ocean waters and demolished adobe huts and brick buildings..."

However, Peru was not the only country in South America to suffer quakes. Again the *El Paso Herald-Post* reported on June 15, 1975:

VIOLENT EARTHQUAKE HITS CENTRAL CHILE

Fortunately there were no serious consequences.

The Virginian-Pilot of Norfolk, Virginia, reported on November 17, 1977:

70 DEAD IN ARGENTINE QUAKE

"Buenos Aires, Argentina (AP)—A powerful earthquake jolted western Argentina early Wednesday, killing at least 70 people, injuring hundreds, and demolishing thousands of dwellings, the military government reported.

"Vice Adm. Julio Bardi, social welfare minister and director of quake relief operations, said the official casualty toll is 70 dead and 254 injured, with at least 10,000 people left homeless.

"The tremors were felt over a wide area reaching into Chile, Peru and Brazil, but serious damage and casualties were reported only in Argentina."

And on the 23rd of November, 1977, the *El Paso Herald-Post* reported:

DEADLY QUAKE HITS SOUTH AMERICA

(Notice the range of this quake):

"Buenos Aires, Argentina (UPI)—A major earthquake rocked Chile, Argentina, and southern Brazil today, severely damaging towns in the Andes mountain foothills. The Argentine government said at least 50 persons were killed and hundreds injured.

"The center of the quake was located near the Argentine city of San Juan, 785 miles northwest of Buenos Aires, near the Chilean border. The intensity of the quake was registered by observatories at between 7.3 and 8.2 on the Richter scale."

As we go to press with this book, the following appeared in the *Virginian-Pilot* on December 13, 1979:

Quake Kills At Least 133 In Colombia

BOGOTA, Colombia (AP)—A powerful earthquake rolling through the Colombia-Ecuador border before dawn Wednesday leveled homes and touched off tidal waves, killing at least 133 people and injuring as many as 2,000 officials said.

Rescue teams said searchers were probing rubble in six flattened southern Colombian coastal cities. They said between 200 and 2,000 people were reported missing.

The Colombia Red Cross declared the entire southwest coast a disaster area and President Julio Cesar Turbay ordered the army to begin rescue operations.

The quake, centered just off the Pacific coast near the border, was measured from 7.8 to 8.1 on the Richter scale and lasted from 2:59 a.m. until 3:04 a.m.

It sent 10-foot-high tidal waves crashing into the shore, causing flooding during the 10 aftershocks that followed during the next hour, said officials with the governor's office in the southern state of Narino.

There seems little doubt that Edgar Cayce had seen some kind of pattern decades ahead of the awesome events.

In 1941 on August 13th, Cayce made some predictions of a general nature in an individual's reading.

As conditions in the geography of the world, of the country— changes here are gradually coming about.

No wonder, then, that the entity feels the need, the necessity for change of central location. For, many portions of the east coast will be disturbed, as well as many portions of the west coast, as well as the central portion of the U.S.

1152-11, Aug. 13, 1941

"... *portions of the east coast.* ..."

The *New York Mirror* in 1948, carried a warning from Dr. L. Don Leet, a professor of seismology, for the New York City area. The heading read:

Scientist Warns N.Y. of Possible Quake

The article opens with the following paragraphs:

"A Harvard scientist warned last week that New York may suffer a severe quake in the near future.

"The scientist, Dr. L. Don Leet, professor of seismology, advised preparations should be made to combat the possible emergency and avoid the disasters of West Coast cities in the past.

"Admitting that some seismologists may disagree with him, Dr. Leet says the present epoch of increasing quakes has not yet passed a climax."

QUAKE ROCKS EAST COAST, NORTH PACIFIC AREA

was a heading in *The Virginian-Pilot* on March 1, 1973. The article's first paragraphs read:

"An earthquake startled millions of residents out of their sleep in eastern Pennsylvania and parts of New Jersey, Delaware, and Maryland Wednesday, several hours after a major quake shook the Kuril Islands in the Northern Pacific.

"There were no injuries reported as a result of the East Coast tremors which triggered an avalanche of phone calls to police and fire department switchboards. The quake. . .rattled windows and caused phones to leap off their cradles. . ."

This was a 3.5 quake on the Richter scale. And on January 31, 1979, the *New York Daily News* carried an article headed:

QUAKE JOLTS JERSEY AND 2 BOROUGHS

"The strongest earthquake to strike the metropolitan area in more than 50 years rocked central New Jersey, Brooklyn and Staten Island yesterday, causing little damage and no injuries but rattling windows as far east as Long Island.

"It was the first time in memory that tremors had been felt within the five boroughs, according to experts at Columbia University's Lamont-Doherty Geological Observatory in Palisades, N.Y."

The *New York Post* reported this incident the same day with the caption:

EARTHQUAKE HERE SHAKES UP SCIENTIST

The article warns of the danger involving nuclear plants:

"Yesterday's tremor here triggered warnings anew of a potential

5

earthquake disaster on the Ramapo Fault near three nuclear power plants in Westchester.

"A scientist at Columbia University's Lamont-Doherty Geological Observatory said that since April when the seismologists and Con Edison clashed over a Columbia report, there have been three earthquakes on the fault."

Man has added to his many concerns with the construction of nuclear plants near earthquake faults.

In August, 1941, an Edgar Cayce reading stated, "Portions of the now east coast of New York, or New York City itself, will in the main disappear. This will be another generation, though, here; *while the southern* portions of Carolina, Georgia—these will disappear. This will be much sooner." [Author's italics] (1152-11, Aug. 13, 1941)

On November 15, 1976, *The Virginian-Pilot* of Norfolk, Virginia, carried an historical report of earthquakes in the Carolinas. The heading read:

CAUSES OF CAROLINA QUAKES STILL A QUESTION TO SCIENCE

The article goes on:

"The Carolinas trembled and 80 people died during the great Charleston earthquake. Ninety years later, scientists say the causes of the Charleston quake and others that have jarred the Carolinas remain a mystery.

"Hundreds of smaller quakes, some sharp jolts causing minor damage, have struck the Carolinas since the large one on Aug. 31, 1886, just a tick of time ago to geophysicists.

"And scientists say if a quake of that magnitude hit today, death and devastation would be vastly greater because of man-made structures. Add to that the proliferation of nuclear power plants, and the potential danger is enough to concern federal agencies such as the U.S. Geological Survey and the Nuclear Regulatory Commission."

And on January 19, 1977, a short article in *The Virginian-Pilot* was headed:

TREMOR SCARES S.C. AREA

The first two paragraphs of the story read:

"Summerville, S.C. (AP)—A tremor shocked the earthquake-prone Summerville area just before 1:30 p.m. Tuesday, causing no damage but, according to a sheriff's department official, scaring the 'the hell' out of residents.

"The U.S. Geological Survey's David Shimp said in Charleston that the tremor registered 3.0 on the Richter Scale at 1:29:19 and was centered between Summerville and St. George, about 25 miles northeast of Charleston."

While the Coast and Geodetic surveys of 1915, 1933, 1935 and 1955 indicate that most of the land surface has subsided as much as 4 inches in the Savannah, Georgia, area—caused apparently by the withdrawal of ground water—and there have been reported earthquakes, these do not seem drastic enough to comply with the prediction. Is this a mistaken psychic perception of time? Are we to expect changes there in the years ahead?

". . . the central portion of the U.S."

On the 5th of January, 1976, *The New York Times* took note of an earth tremor in Missouri. It registered only 3.6 on the Richter scale in two counties in southeast Missouri. However, this was not an isolated incident, and earthquakes in the past in this area have been of much greater magnitude.

"Middle America's Fault" was the title of an article appearing in the Science section of *Time* magazine, Nov. 19, 1979. Three times, the article reported, major earthquakes hit the region around the Mississippi River town of New Madrid, in southeast Missouri, between December 16, 1811, and February 7, 1812. From the survivors' descriptions it is estimated that the quakes' intensities would have had a 7.3-7.5 range on the Richter scale.

"The trio of quakes has another distinction. Most major quakes occur around the boundaries of the great moving plates that form the earth's outer layers. . .Yet the New Madrid area lies in the very heart of the North American plate, far from its boundaries. Why should it have shaken so violently in the early 1800s and, in fact, continued to quiver occasionally ever since?"

With the help of oil-exploration equipment seismologists have concluded that some time in the past the rock had been uplifted (perhaps by volcanism), then collapsed after it cooled, creating sharp breaks which were covered over by the soft sediments of the Mississippi River Valley. Today the underground rift, according to St. Louis University researchers, becomes squeezed whenever the North American plate moves, causing a horizontal movement along the fault line.

". . . portions of the west coast. . ."

In 1936 a 50-year-old man asked Edgar Cayce, "Will San Francisco suffer from such a catastrophe [earthquake] this year?" The answer was:

We do not find that this particular district (San Francisco) in the present year will suffer the great material damages that *have* been experienced heretofore. While portions of the country will be affected, we find these will be farther *east* than San Francisco—or those *south* where there has *not* been heretofore the greater activity.   270-35, Jan. 21, 1936

No strong shock was felt in all of California in 1936, the year of the above reading (U.S. Coast and Geodetic Survey, 1951, p. 30). Published records (*ibid.*, pp. 30-35) indicate that all of the eight principal shocks in California and Nevada, for the period 1936 to 1950, were to the *southeast* of San Francisco.

On August 17, 1969, *The State* and the *Columbia Record,* Columbia, South Carolina, printed an article which recalled in some detail a description of the Yellowstone Park quake of ten years earlier. The heading on this article was:

ONE OF STRONGEST QUAKES STRUCK WITHOUT WARNING

Since the area is northeast of San Francisco and is described as "One of the strongest earthquakes ever recorded in North America," it may be interesting to consider this description carefully. Major extracts follow:

"West Yellowstone, Mont. (AP)—The breeze whispered through the pine trees and stars twinkled in the clear sky while about 250 campers slept in the Madison River Canyon in southwestern Montana.

"Without warning, an awesome roar split the night. The earth heaved and rolled. Fissures opened in the earth's crust. A 7,600-foot mountain cracked and part of it fell into the canyon, generating hurricane-force winds that scattered cars, people and camp trailers.

" 'I thought the world was coming to an end,' recalls Mrs. George Hungerford, of the massive earthquake that jolted an eight-state area 10 years ago at 11:37 p.m. on August 17, 1959.

"The quake, one of the strongest ever recorded in North America, left 28 dead, including 19 who were buried, perhaps for eternity, under an estimated 30 million tons of rock.

"The Hungerfords have lived in the canyon 13 years. He is keeper of the Montana Power Company's Hebgen Dam, which backs up 345,000 acre-feet of water. Reports immediately following the quake erroneously indicated the dam had broken, sending a wave of terror through the downstream valley and resulting in evacuation of the town of Ennis.

"Geologists say that within 60 seconds of the first shock, 40 million cubic yards of rock fell from the shattered mountain into the canyon. The avalanche covered the bottom of the canyon to a height of about 200 feet and continued about 400 feet up the canyon's opposite side.

"The slide blocked the Madison River with a dam that would have taken years for man to build.

"Campers who survived the slide were left dazed and bleeding. Many of them had their clothing torn from them by avalanche winds.

"Those who tried to flee found all exits blocked. One end of the highway was buried under the avalanche and sections of the road on the other end of the canyon had fallen into Hebgen Reservoir.

"Upstream at Hebgen Dam, water was sloshing back and forth from one end of the reservoir to the other. Hungerford says he checked the dam soon after the first shock and found it intact. But, he says, there appeared to be no water in the reservoir.

"Some minutes later water rushed back toward the dam and tumbled over the top.

"The back-and-forth surges continued for hours but, despite the hydraulic pressure and repeated earth shocks, the dam held.

"When the lake quieted, it was obvious the far end of the reservoir had been raised and the land on the dammed end had dropped about nine feet.

"The quake measured 7.1 on the Richter scale, compared with the 8.2 magnitude of the 1906 San Francisco earthquake.

"People stayed in San Francisco and rebuilt their city, but of those living in the Madison Canyon 10 years ago, the Hungerfords are about the only ones still there."

Today scientists as well as psychics are predicting California quakes. Let's look at a few of the stream of articles which have been appearing for some time now. *The Virginian-Pilot* and *The Portsmouth Star* on April 15, 1956, carried an article titled "San Francisco Sits on an Earthquake—Simply Waiting for It to Go Off!" Dr. Charles Richter and Dr. Hugo Benioff of California Institute of Technology are quoted as follows:

"Dr. Charles Richter, of California Institute of Technology, says seismologists would need accurate records for a thousand years before attempting to predict earthquakes with even partial accuracy. He feels California may go 10 years more without a San Andreas quake—but one could come tomorrow.

"It is his personal belief that the most likely place for the next big quake is in the area of Fort Tejon, on the ridge route between Bakersfield and Los Angeles. This is because there has been 'no movement of consequence' in that area since a great tremor in 1857.

"Dr. Hugo Benioff, another Cal-Tech expert, told a recent meeting of the National Academy of Science that he believes the next big San Andreas quake will be between San Luis Obispo and San Benito counties. This is a long stretch of the fault line which was not disturbed in either 1857 or 1906. Referring to this section, Benioff told newsmen, 'I'm surprised it hasn't happened already.' "

"Major Quake Predicted on San Andreas Fault" was the headline in a San Jose paper on July 8, 1968. The article included the following:

"California scientists have been successful in predicting one or more past earthquakes and are now predicting 'major movements' on the San Andreas Fault.

"The major movements 'can be expected' along a 250-mile stretch of the San Andreas between Cholame in San Luis Obispo County and San Bernardino, according to a new report released by the State Department of Water Resources."

The Oregon Journal, Portland, Oregon, carried an article on February 10, 1971, "Scientists Say Worse Quake Certain in California." In part the article reads:

"The earthquake that shook the Los Angeles area Tuesday occurred on a branch of the 650-mile San Andreas Fault along which masses of Californians continue to live and build new homes.

"Scientists have warned again and again of the dangers of new quakes.

"A quake the size of San Francisco's 1906 disaster—measuring 8.3 on the Richter Scale—is considered 'inevitable' on the San Andreas Fault by Dr. William Pecora, director of the U.S. Geological Survey and numerous others.

"Such a quake would be roughly 1,000 times more powerful than Tuesday's shaking of the San Gabriel Fault, a branch of the San Andreas. Its force would be on the rough equivalent of 5 million tons of TNT."

The quake referred to in the clipping above was described in part in the *San Jose Mercury-News,* February 14, 1971, as follows: "62 Killed, 1,000 Injured in L.A. Earthquake." The report continues:

"The worst earthquake since 1933 rumbled through Southern California last week.

"It struck a massive blow that left at least 62 persons dead, more than 1,000 injured and more than a billion dollars in damage.

"Tens of thousands of people were evacuated from a section of the sprawling San Fernando Valley beneath a threatened dam.

"Buildings collapsed at two hospitals, accounting for more than half the death toll.

"Twelve freeway overpass bridges fell into freeway lanes. One killed two men, crushing their pickup truck liked a stepped-on toy.

"Broken gas lines touched off hundreds of fires. Aftershocks continued through the afternoon.

"The big temblor, measuring 6.5 on the Richter Scale, was centered 26 miles northwest of Los Angeles near Newhall.

"It hit hardest at the north end of the San Fernando Valley, where 1.3 million persons live."

The *San Jose Mercury-News* carried another comment on August 26, 1971, on the possible seriousness of the quakes ahead:

MAJOR QUAKE MAY HIT MOUNTAINS ANY TIME

A state geologist, Thomas H. Rogers, is quoted:

"A major earthquake along the San Andreas Fault could spell disaster for people and structures in the Santa Cruz Mountains, a state geologist told county officials yesterday.

" 'The fault is not moving now,' Thomas H. Rogers, of the State Division of Mines and Geology, told the board of supervisors 'but that doesn't mean it won't move at any minute.'

" 'In fact there's one theory that since it hasn't moved this means it will move again in a major earthquake,' Rogers said."

On August 12, 1979, *The New York Times* carried this item:

"For about 10 seconds last week, California was on the move again. At 10:05 a.m. Monday a region stretching from San Francisco southwards was hit by its strongest earthquake in 68 years. The quake was measured at different intensities by different seismographic stations, but at an average value of about 5.9 on the Richter Scale, compared with 6.6 for the last big quake in 1911 and 8.3 for the great

11

San Francisco earthquake of 1906 (on the Richter Scale, each whole number represents a tenfold increase in intensity; thus, 8.3 is 100 times as violent as 6.3). No injuries were reported, but being scared was widespread."

On Wednesday, October 17, 1979, *The Virginian-Pilot* of Norfolk, Va., carried the following front-page article:

CALIFORNIA FAULT SHAKES FOR 2ND DAY

"El Centro, Calif.—California Gov. Edmund G. Brown, Jr., declared a state of emergency Tuesday in Imperial County as aftershocks to the biggest earthquake in California in eight years shivered down the Imperial Fault and the number of injured climbed to nearly 100.

"Damage rocketed into the millions of dollars.

"Although damage to public facilities alone was estimated at $15 million and damage to privately owned buildings will push the total higher, there were few serious injuries in the earthquake which shook Southern California and northern Mexico at 4:16 p.m. (PDT) Monday. It registered 6.4 on the Richter Scale."

As disturbing was the report of the recent tidal wave in the Mediterranean which occurred on October 17, 1979, coinciding or just following the earthquake on that same date on the California-Mexican border.

From *The Virginian-Pilot*, Norfolk, Va., October 18, 1979:

RIVIERA TIDAL WAVE LEAVES DISASTER AREA

"Nice, France (AP)—The Riviera coast was declared a disaster area Wednesday by the French government, which began an inquiry to determine the cause of the Mediterranean tidal wave that killed 11 people, wrecked countless pleasure craft, and caused at least $10 million damage."

Activity in the Mediterranean area was related to California earthquakes in a 1936 reading. This reading, dealing with volcanoes, was unusual because it specified a time frame for certain events.

If there are the greater activities in Vesuvius, or Pelée, then the southern coast of California—and the areas between Salt Lake and the southern portions of Nevada—may expect within the three months following same, an inundation by the earthquakes.   **270-35, Jan. 21, 1936**

A major eruption of Vesuvius, a volcano dominating the Bay of Naples in Italy, destroyed most of Pompeii, Herculaneum and Stabiae in 79 A.D. There was a big eruption in 1139 and a major one in 1631 when fifteen towns were wrecked. Over 16,000 people died in 79 A.D., only 4,000 in 1631. Minor eruptions have taken place in 1779, 1793, 1872, 1906 and 1944.

The major eruption of Mount Pelée on Martinique in the West Indies took place in 1902, killing some 30,000 people. A severe eruption, which lasted 3 years, began in 1929.

Are these destructive volcanoes related to very deep geological formations associated with the earthquake faults in California? These events are the only indications of a time for serious California quakes other than a reference in reading 1152-11, dated August 13, 1941. This states that Los Angeles and San Francisco will suffer before New York City which would not be destroyed before another generation.

Remember, the Edgar Cayce readings which have just been quoted were given in 1936 and 1941. Apparently there is good reason to watch Vesuvius and Pelée. It was not reassuring to read in the *Washington Daily News* of March 7, 1960, "Vesuvius Is Getting Ready to Blow Its Top Again." The article quoted Professor Eduardo Vittozzi, seismologist of the Vesuvius Observatory who lectures at Naples University. In answer to a question as to how soon an eruption would take place, he said:

"Ours is not an exact science. But of this we are convinced: when the next eruption comes it will be a major one. The volcano has been quiet for too long. Past experience shows that to be a bad sign. Always when there is a long spell of quiet the eruption that follows is the more violent."

Another clipping adds a further disturbing reminder. The *El Paso Herald-Post* carried the following headline on September 28, 1965:

Vesuvius Was Worst of Killer Volcanoes

We took note, too, of a short article in *The Virginian-Pilot*, December 6, 1971, "Volcano Pelée Starts Steaming." The article goes on:

"Christiansted, St. Croix, V.I. (UP)—Mount Pelée, one of the world's deadliest volcanoes, began steaming today on the French Caribbean island of Martinique after almost 70 years of sleep."

Pelée is a sister volcano to Mount Soufriere, on the British associated state island of St. Vincent, which is believed by scientists to be near eruption.

In May, 1902, the two volcanoes erupted almost simultaneously, with Pelée wiping out a city of 30,000 persons and Soufriere taking another 2,000 lives.

The Jupiter Effect

And finally, an interesting article appeared in *The National Insider,* November 10, 1974:

IT'LL HAPPEN IN 1982, ASTROPHYSICISTS SAY
2 SCIENTISTS WARN RARE MOVEMENT OF PLANETS WILL CAUSE DESTRUCTION OF LOS ANGELES BY EARTHQUAKE

"An unusual alignment of the planets in our solar system will cause Los Angeles to be destroyed by earthquake in 1982, two scientists claim.

"The alignment will be such that it will create huge storms on the surface of the sun that will disrupt radio communications and weather on earth before triggering catastrophic tremors.

"This is the belief set forth by astrophysicists Dr. John R. Gribbin and Dr. Stephen Plagemann in their new book, *The Jupiter Effect,* published by Walker and Company.

" 'The alignments of the planets can, for sound scientific reasons, affect the behavior of the earth,' they noted.

" 'The gravity of the planets can affect the sun through tidal interactions. Disturbances on the sun can influence the earth through changes in the magnetic field, which links all the planets in the solar system.

" 'Only on very rare occasions can these small effects add up to produce any dramatic results on earth,' Gribbin and Plagemann said. 'But one of these occasions—an alignment of the planets that occurs only once every 179 years—is due in 1982.

" 'We are convinced this will trigger off regions of earthquake activity on earth. By that time, the Californian San Andreas Fault system will be under considerable accumulated strain.

" 'Geophysicists report that their measurements of the fault now show it is overdue for a slip greater than that of 1906, and just needs a trigger.

" 'There can be little doubt that the planetary and solar influence in the early 1980s, following the rare planetary alignment, will provide that trigger.' "

I am reasonably sure that such a report has been the stimulus for a number of "psychic" reports of upheavals in the early 1980s. Sensitives often pick up thought-form impressions (mass thought patterns) which to them are very real. Yet I must remind myself that Edgar Cayce's reference (quoted at the beginning of this chapter) to the position of Jupiter and Uranus led to a very accurate prediction of events two months in the future in various parts of the world. (195-32) We must, it seems to me, try to come to a better understanding of the "thought world" created by man which has an influence on earth movements. As Cayce pointed out, "Tendencies in the hearts and souls of men are such that these upheavals may be brought about." (416-7, Oct. 7, 1935)

Chapter II

LANDS SINKING, LANDS RISING

Disturbances in Japan

Reading 3976-15 given in 1934 included in its statements the prediction that "The greater portion of Japan must go into the sea."

Japan is geologically unstable, lying in that area called the "Ring of Fire" (the circumpacific belt) along which the greater number of the world's earthquakes take place. It is crisscrossed by major fault systems and has a frightening record of disasters. Twenty-seven thousand people were killed by an earthquake-caused tidal wave in 1896. One hundred and forty-three thousand were destroyed by an earthquake and tidal wave in 1923. Throughout its history Japan and the seas around it have been subject to the most severe earthquakes. Recent headlines from our files show that the pattern is continuing.

POWERFUL QUAKE ROCKS JAPAN ISLE
Norfolk Ledger Dispatch
March 4, 1952

JAPAN ROCKED—HUGE SEA QUAKE
Chicago Daily News
August 12, 1969

TOKYO WARNED OF QUAKE IN FEW YEARS
Urged to Create Parks, Curb Oil Fires
Philadelphia Inquirer
September 7, 1972

DEVASTATING QUAKE FORESEEN IN JAPAN
Scottsdale Daily Progress
December 9, 1976

AT LEAST 21 DIE IN JAPANESE QUAKE
Philadelphia Inquirer
June 13, 1978

TOKYO IN DANGER OF DESTRUCTION
Spotlight, Washington, D.C.
December 4, 1978

The Japanese govenment, aware of the danger to the island, supports earthquake research. Monitoring systems now exist across the country and regular earthquake drills take place.

Ancient Lands

One of the most controversial subjects dealt with in the Edgar Cayce psychic data is Atlantis, supposedly an ancient continent formerly in the Atlantic Ocean. This land, according to Cayce, was broken up by a series of earthquakes. One of the last islands was called Poseidia. In one individual's life reading the following was given:

And Poseidia will be among the first portions of Atlantis to rise again. Expect it in sixty-eight and sixty-nine, not so far away. 955-3, June 28, 1940

That mention of a specific date for an earth movement is rarely found in the Edgar Cayce readings. Was Cayce wrong? Undersea explorations in progress since the '60s have shed new light on an old "myth."

Underwater structures were uncovered by shifting sands between Bimini and the Andros Islands off the Florida coast in 1968. These were man-made, as were artifacts picked up off Bimini, an island off the Florida coast, in the same year. These have not been dated nor identified as of Atlantean origin. However, another impressive report appeared early in 1970, in a Miami, Florida, paper under the heading: "Fabled Atlantis Found? Caribbean Area Granite a Clue." The date of the article suggests that the actual dredging occurred in 1969. The article contains such fascinating details that it is reprinted here in its entirety.

FABLED ATLANTIS FOUND?
Caribbean Area Granite a Clue
by Richard Pothier
Herald Science Writer

"Scientists aboard a Duke University research ship docked in Miami Friday with evidence of a possible 'lost continent' or a brand-new continental mass in the south Caribbean.

"The evidence, more than a ton of granite-type continental rocks, was dredged up in thousands of feet of water on the open ocean floor between the Virgin Islands and Venezuela.

" 'The rocks indicate either that a lost continent once rose from these waters or that nature is now building a new continental mass in the area,' scientists said.

"No matter which theory the discovery eventually supports, recovery of the granite material so far from land is considered a geological find of major, worldwide significance.

"*Eastward,* Duke's 117-foot research ship, pulled into Miami early Friday after a three-month marine geological expedition through the Caribbean. The granite rock was recovered from more than 50 locations on the Aves Ridge, which runs north and south from Venezuela to the Virgin Islands.

"Scientists and geology students aboard, all from Columbia University's Lamont-Doherty Geological Observatory, said such rocks have never been recovered before from the open ocean floor.

"Dr. Bruce C. Heezen, chief scientist aboard the *Eastward* on the National Science Foundation-supported cruise, said the discoveries have 'wide geological implications.'

" 'Up to now, geologists generally believed that light granite, or acid igneous, rocks are confined to the continents and that the crust of the earth beneath the sea is composed of heavier, dark-colored basaltic rock,' Dr. Heezen said.

" 'Thus, the occurrence of light-colored granitic rocks may support an old theory that a continent formerly existed in the region of the eastern Caribbean and that these rocks may represent the core of a subsided lost continent.'

"The rocks themselves were taken off the *Eastward* at Key West and shipped to Columbia for more analysis, including radioactive dating tests.

"Dr. C.G. Bookhout, acting director of Duke's multi-college research program, said the finds were 'very, very exciting.' More analysis will be needed before the ultimate implications of the rock samples become clear, he said.

"Another nationally known marine geologist, Dr. Robert Dietz of the Environmental Science Services Administration's Miami-based laboratories, said he believed the existence of light, granitic rocks in open-floor areas of the Caribbean probably indicates that new continental material is being forced up through the surface of the earth.

" 'If these rocks are eventually found to be less than 100 to 150 million years old, I believe that will be the answer. The find is quite significant, certainly, even if it doesn't turn out to support this "lost continent" theory,' he said.

"Dr. Dietz, one of the geologists responsible for the modern concepts of continental drift and sea-floor spreading, said the *Eastward's* discoveries will probably add to the mounting evidence that the continents are spreading apart through 'sea-floor spreading' mechanisms deep within the earth.

" 'We think the area where they recovered these rocks is one of the regions where the earth's crust is going down, to offset the emergence of new material at the mid-Atlantic Ridge. If this is the case, such fusible rocks as granite should be coming up again in the same regions.' "

Well after the key 1968-69 dates mentioned by Cayce in 1940, other reports continue to keep this teasing riddle, fable or fact in people's consciousnesses.

On March 17, 1970, *The Miami Herald* headlines an article on the Caribbean with:

CORAL FOSSILS SUGGEST CARIBBEAN MAY BE LONG-SUNKEN CONTINENT

"Geologists have found evidence that a 5-mile-deep trench in the Caribbean may once have been dry land, suggesting that much of the Caribbean may be a long-sunken 'lost continent.'

"A team of Columbia University scientists reported Monday that it recently found remains of shallow-water life in rock under 25,000 feet of water near the eastern end of the Dominican Republic.

"The scientists, Dr. Bruce C. Heezen and Paul J. Fox, said they'd come to the 'remarkable conclusion that the deepest portion of the Atlantic Ocean was once coral reef-bordered land.'

" 'Coral reefs don't grow at depths of more than 50 feet,' Dr. Heezen said. 'This means the area we studied once had to be near sea level.' "

And on July 27, 1975, the *Philadelphia Inquirer* reported:

SUNKEN REMAINS OF OLD CONTINENT FOUND IN ATLANTIC

"Miami—A group of international oceanographers say it has discovered the remains of a continent sunken thousands of feet in the middle of the Atlantic Ocean.

"The scientists attributed their discovery to bits of fossilized crab excrement and pieces of ancient limestone.

"The samples were dredged up from 1,700 to 3,000 feet below the sea surface during an expedition several years ago [1969?]. The evidence was found in a fracture zone of the Mid-Atlantic Ridge, a giant,

19

undersea mountain range that encircles the globe and runs continuously through all major ocean basins."

One of the latest, though meager, reports of a new discovery of Atlantis appeared in a small notice released by the Russians who claimed that they discovered standing columns and steps hundreds of feet under water off the Azores. If they do indeed release pictures of this find, it may prove of great importance.

In a newspaper interview published in *The Virginian-Pilot* and *The Ledger-Star,* September 28, 1979, Egerton Sykes, recognized as one of the world's most foremost authorities on Atlantis, said, "The Russians, six weeks ago, said they discovered the first piece of concrete evidence of Atlantis: a wall and staircase built into a mountain range 300 feet beneath the surface of the ocean. They believe it is part of the ancient civilization."

Sykes believes it is the proof he has been searching for. "Nature can build walls but nature never built a staircase, neatly cut steps," he said. "This is the first bit of real proof we've had in my lifetime, on the existence of the lost continent of Atlantis."

Lands in the Pacific

So much material was given in the Cayce readings on Atlantis that the indexed references to a sunken continent in the *Pacific* are generally ignored. One such reference reads, "Before this we find the entity in that land now known as the American, during the periods when the Lemurian or the lands of Mu or Zu were being in their turmoils for destruction." (509-1, Feb. 3, 1934)

There are indications from the references to Mu in the readings that the Pacific continent was destroyed before the final island of Atlantis disappeared: ". . .by the convulsive movements which came about in the earth through the destruction of Lemuria, Atlantis and in later periods—the flood." (281-42, Nov. 1, 1939)

On June 6, 1977, *The Houston Post* carried an article under the heading: "Geophysicist Claims 2nd Lost Continent Dispersed in Pacific."

The article contained the following paragraphs:

"Washington (AP)—Atlantis may not be the only lost continent.

Scientists say there could have been another in the Pacific Ocean and that its breakup may have created several major mountain ranges, including the Rockies and the Andes.

"But Amos Nur, a Stanford University geophysicist, said Friday that there is indirect evidence that a continent slightly smaller than Australia began breaking up about 200 million years ago and that major fragments became embedded in other continental masses about 80 million years later after fanning out over the Pacific.

"Nur told the annual meeting of the American Geophysical Union that the Pacifica fragments could have created the great mountain ranges bordering the Pacific Ocean when they slammed into North and South America, Alaska, Northeastern Russia, Japan and East Asia."

New Land Rising

The lengthy article by Richard Pothier, quoted earlier, referred in the last paragraph to the possibility of granite rocks "coming up again in the same regions [Atlantic]." In a reading given on August 13, 1941, Cayce stated:

In the next few years lands will appear in the Atlantic as well as in the Pacific.   1152-11

The following extracts give evidence of these occurrences. On October 31, 1965, the *San Jose Mercury-News* reported:

NEW ISLAND EXCITES SCIENTISTS

The article goes on to state:

"Moffett Field—With a mighty heave and a loud gasp, Mother Earth gave forth a new child on a cold November morning in 1963.

"An island suddenly sprang up in the Atlantic Ocean near Iceland.

"Propelled by mighty volcanic forces deep in the bowels of the earth, a rocky point jutted up through the frigid sea and grew until it spanned more than two miles.

"Icelanders called it 'Surtsey' for an ancient Norse god of fire.

"Two delighted scientists here who recently trampled over the rocky volcanic isle are calling it an exciting sample of earth as it existed billions of years ago.

" 'And,' say Drs. Richard Young and Cyril Ponnamperuma of Ames Research Center, 'it may help teach us how, eons ago, life began on Earth.' "

The Virginian-Pilot of Norfolk, Va., reported on March 3, 1960:

Island Born Off Coast of Ecuador

"Quito, Ecuador (AP)—An island more than a mile long, 100 yards wide and as high as 125 feet at some points has emerged from the Pacific off the coast of Ecuador.

"Two eyewitnesses to the island's birth on Sunday said it was heralded by trembling of the earth and strange underground noises. The location is 36 miles north of Carraquez Bay in Manabi Province.

"Walter Camacho, director of the Coastal Polytechnical School, investigated their story and Friday confirmed the island's birth. He said it was formed of clay and calcareous rocks which apparently pushed their way out of the sea during contraction of upper geological seabed strata."

On February 13, 1972, the *San Jose Mercury-News* carried an inch-high caption for a story on two northeast mountains rising out of the Pacific:

Two Islands Rising Toward Birth Out of Pacific

"Washington (UPI)—Scientists Saturday reported signs that two submerged mountains in the northeast Pacific are slowly rising and may eventually lift their summits above the water as new islands."

". . . in the South Sea. . .and the Etna area. . ."

Q-12. How soon will the changes in the earth's activity begin to be apparent?
A-12. When there is the first breaking up of some conditions in the South Sea (that's South Pacific, to be sure), and those as apparent in the sinking or rising of that that's almost opposite same, or in the Mediterranean, and the Etna area, then we may know it has begun.   311-8, April 9, 1932

News stories published on the same day in September, 1979, no longer seem like coincidences.

From *The Virginian-Pilot,* Norfolk, Virginia, September 13, 1979:

"Jakarta, Indonesia (AP)—An earthquake measuring 8.0 on the Richter Scale rocked the eastern tip of the Indonesian province of Irian Jaya on Wednesday, destroying half the houses in one town, 2,300 miles east of here, officials said.

"Interior Department spokesman Faisal Tamin said there was no immediate word on the fate of the 8,000 residents in the devastated

22

town of Ansus.

"Tamin said major damage also was reported in the town of Serui."

From the *Memphis Star,* also on September 13, 1979:

9 TOURISTS DIE IN ETNA ERUPTION

"Catania, Sicily—Mount Etna erupted like a cannon, showering fiery lava on 200 tourists and killing nine of them in the first deaths on the slopes of the storied volcano since 1842.

"The bodies of three victims were not immediately identified. The other six persons killed in the Wednesday evening eruption were all Italians, including three physicians who were attending a medical congress in Sicily.

"Search operations, suspended because of darkness Wednesday night, resumed at dawn today. Police said they feared the death toll might go higher as rescuers probed a mass of rocks near the lip of the crater."

We can see that the readings have apparently pinpointed a link between two areas of seismic activity—a link that is an indication of earth changes to come.

The numerous news articles quoted have certainly shown that the earth is on the move and in patterns predicted by the readings.

Prophecies that failed?

It is fair at this point to consider some of the Edgar Cayce readings on prophecy which are confusing and seem to have been inaccurate. On February 13, 1933, Cayce was asked this question: "Will the upheavals during 1936 affect San Francisco as it did in 1906?" He answered, "This'll be a baby beside what it'll be in '36." (270-30) The 1969 World Almanac lists the San Francisco quake of 1906. There is no major quake listed for 1936.

June 12, 1934—a Cayce reading contains this question and answer:

Q-20. Are details of the Earth's eruptions in 1936 so fixed that you can give me an outline of the Pacific Coast area to be affected, along with precautionary measures to be exercised during and after this catastrophe?

A-20. All of these are, as is ever on or in such an activity, dependent upon individuals or groups who are in or keep an attitude respecting the needs, the desires, the necessary requirements in such a field of activity. That some are *due* and *will* occur is *written,* as it were, but—as we find it—as to specific date or time at present this may not be given.

270-32, June 12, 1934

Then on January 21, 1936, as has been noted, the Cayce data indicated that there would be no serious quake in San Francisco, but rather farther east. This was correct but it is a direct refutation of the February, 1933, statement. What had changed?

Certainly Edgar Cayce spoke of 1936 as a crucial year. On February 8, 1932, he stated (3976-10) in answer to a question, "Please forecast the principal events for the next fifty years affecting the welfare of the human race": "This had best be cast after the great catastrophe that's coming to the world in '36 in the form of the breaking up of many powers that now exist as factors in world affairs...Then with the breaking up in '36 will be the changes that will make different maps of the world." Was Cayce referring here to Hitler's repudiation of the Versailles treaty and reparations agreement, as well as the remilitarization of the Rhineland in 1936? This was a different kind of upheaval leading to World War II.

However, this same reading goes on in answer to a question on the form of government in Italy to mention 1936 in a different way. "These will not come as we find, as broken, before the catastrophes of outside forces to the earth in '36, which will come from the shifting of the equilibrium of the earth itself *in* space with those of the consequential effects upon the various positions of the. . .world affected by same."

On July 1, 1932, a further question on '36 brought this answer:

"What will be the type and extent of the upheaval in '36?" Answer: "The wars, the upheavals in the interior of the earth, and the shifting of same by the differentiation in the axis as respecting the positions from the Polaris center." (5748-6)

In writing about this matter in 1960 (see Part II, p. 84), a geologist pointed out that these readings were very important in dealing with future predicted earth changes. He referred to T. Gold's discussion of the instability of the earth's axis of rotation in *Nature,* Vol. 175, and to Elsasser's and Munk's estimate that the geographic pole moved amost 15 feet between 1900 and 1940.[1]

Again in 1932 a question was asked which brought another reference to 1936, which to me doesn't seem to have worked out.

Q-29. Are there to be physical changes in the earth's surface in Alabama?
A-29. Not for some period yet.
Q-30. When will the changes begin?
A-30. Thirty-six to thirty-eight.
Q-31. What part of the State will be affected?
A-31. The northwestern part, and the extreme southwestern part.   311-9, Aug. 6, 1932

Q-14. Are the physical changes in Alabama predicted for 1936-38 to be gradual or sudden changes?
A-14. Gradual.
Q-15. What form will they take?
A-15. To be sure, that may depend upon much that deals with metaphysical as well as what people call actual, or in truth! For as understood—or should be [understood] by the entity—there are those conditions that in the activity of individuals, in line of thought and endeavor, oft keep many a city and many a land intact, through their application of the spiritual laws in their associations with individuals. This will take more of the form here in the change, as we find, through the sinking of portions, with the following-up of the inundations by this overflow.   311-10, Nov. 19, 1932

Apparently we must assume that there were some very positive attitudes developed in Alabama which mitigated the changes. Let us consider what our attitudes toward psychics should involve.

---

[1]Elsasser, W.H. and Munk, W., "Geomagnetic Drift and Rotation of the Earth," pp. 228-236 in Benioff, H., et al, editors. Contributions in geophysics in honor of Beno Gutenberg, 1958, Pergamon Press, p. 224.

Chapter III

OUR ATTITUDES TOWARD PSYCHICS

It is very likely that our media will continue to carry more and more reports of dire happenings as predicted by well-known and little-known psychics. How can we evaluate such data? When do we cancel a plane reservation? When do we pack our bags and move from a so-called "dangerous area"? While this subject won't be explored in all its complexity, it would be wise to recognize some of the major factors which are involved in any type of psychic perception.

The Edgar Cayce readings are very supportive of the concept that we are all psychic. Some of us pay more attention to our telepathic, clairvoyant or precognitive experiences than others. Some individuals begin to use and even depend on such perceptions almost without consciously being aware of it. Psychic ability of any kind must be used if it is to be developed. As we observe our own hunches, dreams, healing experiences or even out-of-body experiences, we should consider the possible sources of any information that is picked up just as carefully as we consider data from gifted sensitives.

First, let's look carefully at the motivations involved in psychic experiences. Our own purposes are sometimes as difficult to analyze as the purposes of others. Is the individual involved, you or others, already convinced that economic chaos, war, social upheavals, and physical destruction in the earth are unavoidable? Any psychic perception will be colored by such concerns. Is an individual seeking attention, power over others, commercial gain? Certainly a laborer is worthy of his hire, but what comes first in terms of the purpose of giving out the information? There is conscious fraud and chicanery, of course, in the field, but many sensitives (including ourselves) fool us as well as others. The ego is indeed a trickster.

Second, we must consider several possible sources of psychic information; some are more reliable than others. The storehouse of our memories which lies below consciousness is far vaster than we realize. It is possible that everything—every sight, smell, sound, touch and taste since birth—is recorded and, under the right condition, can be recalled. All such data can be interjected into psychic perception and seem quite new. The inner windows of our minds called telepathy, clairvoyance, retrocognition and precognition, open onto worlds to which we are attracted by our development in this and other lives. (Let me pause and define development here as "the understanding obtained by the *application* of spiritual laws known to us.")

There is a world of thought forms composed of all the positive and negative, creative and destructive patterns of thought of all mankind. Imagine what a mass of fear patterns are created by a scientific report of coming upheavals in the '80s. Psychic perceptions of such patterns look as real to the undeveloped sensitive as the actual event. Immediately one may say, "But what of the psychic who is in touch with a dead person, or an angelic being?" In my opinion, most of such communications are with the thought forms built by both the sensitive and the individual while in the earth plane. They are not the actual dead person or higher being, in an exact sense. Of course, there are exceptions. How does one sort out the wheat from the chaff? Jesus' admonition, "By their fruits. . ." is the best measure I know. In other words, what is the record of accuracy and the results when the information is tested?

Next, we should consider another factor which requires careful examination of *each* instance of psychic perception. Any reach of the mind can break through time and space during a given experience. For example, Edgar Cayce was given the purported location for a buried treasure in one of the few readings he gave on such subjects. Did we move him to the time and the place as it existed when the treasure was buried hundreds of years ago? By the suggestion did we tune him into the mind patterns of the people who buried the treasure? Many of those who took part in the burial of such treasures were reluctant at the time of placing the cache to reveal its actual location. Confusions of information can result.

Can a sensitive tune in to the pattern of an earthquake or a storm which is set up by the material evolution of the earth coupled with man's influence on such natural patterns? Yes, that too seems possible, but here we must deal finally with a major point of view in the Edgar Cayce data that man influences, for good or bad, the forces of nature itself. This extract from the readings speaks to this point. It was given November 28, 1939:

As in relationship to changes these are indicated not only through prophecies but through astrological aspects, as well as the thought and intent of persons and groups in high places, bringing about these things, these conditions, in what might be said the fullness of time.

However—since the advent of the Son of Man in the earth giving man an advocate with the Father—there has been an influence that may counteract much of that which has been indicated that would come as retribution, or in fulfilling the law of an evolution of ideas and the relationship of material things to the thoughts and intents of individuals and groups.

Then as to whether the hearts and minds of individuals or souls (who were given authority concerning the laws of the universe) are fired with thoughts of dire consequences or those things that bespeak of the greater development of a spiritual awakening is still in the keeping and in the activities of individuals—who, as this entity, have caught a glimpse, or an awareness, of that which is in the making, in the affairs of state, nation, and nations, and the universe as related to the conditions upon the face of Mother Earth.

There enters much then, that might become questions as respecting that which has been foretold, or prophesied as well as respecting the activities of groups and individuals *who have acted and who are to act* as a counterbalance to those happenings in the earth. . .

Again the interpretation of the signs and the omens becomes an individual experience. And each soul—as this entity—then is given the privilege, the opportunity to live such an activity in its relationships to its fellow man—filling, fulfilling, and interpreting that which has been indicated, in such measures and such manners as to bring hope and not fear, peace and not hate, that which is constructive, not destructive, into the lives and minds and hearts of others.   1602-5

A well-known illustration from P.D. Ouspensky, philosopher, mathematician, mystic and student of Gurdjieff, will help clarify the point. A man is fishing on a river bank. Upriver there is a man in a sailboat coming toward him. The boat and its occupant are in the future of the fisherman on the bank. As the boat comes into view, it is in the present of the fisherman; and as it goes around the bend of the river, it disappears into the past.

28

Now consider a pilot in an airplane above the same river. From his point of view, the boat and its occupant are always in a present time in motion. The pilot may be thought of as a sensitive who through altering his state of consciousness has moved, so to speak, in time-space. However, we must also realize that the will, the choice, of the boat's occupant must be taken into consideration. Suppose the boatman decided to land before he appeared in the fisherman's view. In a sense the boat and the man in it never existed for the fisherman, however real it seemed to the pilot, or psychic. What if we stop worrying over an earthquake and begin praying for God's will to be done? What if many pray? Certainly it seems possible that the energies of thought may affect the outcome of any potential event.

How we think, how we apply the spiritual laws which we know at any given point in time-space plays a very important part in the events which lie ahead. Ever since I saw a Russian housewife, Nelya Kulagina, move a small object by willing it to move, ever since I watched Edgar Cayce many years ago heal himself of a deep congestion of the lungs in 20 minutes, I have tried to face more honestly my responsibility for the effects of my thoughts, words and actions on the world in which we live. You and I are responsible for our world and our brothers. What will we determine now to be the future for us all?

Our Attitudes About Earth Changes in the Years Ahead

In 1934, eleven years before his death in 1945, Edgar Cayce spoke of 1958 to 1998 as being years of great change, not just earth changes, but broad economic, social and political changes, as well. He spoke of a new age. After describing some of the changes which we have noted in Japan, the West Coast of America, etc., on January 19, 1934, Cayce said, "And these will begin in those periods in '58 to '98, when these will be proclaimed as the periods when His light will be seen again in the clouds. . ." (3976-15)

Edgar Cayce places the responsibility for our national problems, indeed, our world problems—with man. On November 5, 1933, he stated:

When man has faltered, when man has altered that law and

has deprived others from expressing their birthright. . .then conditions arise which create the fruits of evil influence in the earth. These are hate, jealousy, avarice, and the like. These in turn tend to create other conditions in all walks of life: love of power, love of position, love of money. . .Now since this has been exactly the experience in the affairs of our nation, as a nation, so our nation, as a nation, is going through a period when *each soul must turn within and seek its own relationship to the Creative Forces, within its own experiences.* [Author's italics]   3976-14

In the same series of readings on the 20th and 24th of June, 1938, he pointed out:

It is well understood by some that a new order of conditions is to arise: there must be many a purging in high places as well as in low. . .certain circumstances will come about in political, economic, and *whole relationships,* in which a leveling will occur. . .or a greater comprehension of the need for it.
                                                                    3976-18

For the time or period draws near for such changes to come, with a new order. It behooves all who have an ideal— individuals as well as groups, societies and organizations—to practice faithfully the application of this ideal in their experience and relationships one to another. Unless they are up and doing, indeed there must come a new order for their relationships and activities.   3976-18

We are our brother's keeper. If those in a position to give of their means, wealth, education, and position do not take these truths into consideration, then there must be that leveling which is to come.   3976-19

Of course, in the light of the events of World War II we may consider that man has paid his debt at least to some extent for his greed, lust for power and mistreatment of his fellow man; and certainly the average man of today does not accept any personal responsibility for these wars nor for those which followed. In my opinion, this is not Edgar Cayce's position. To the degree that each one of us holds animosity, fear, jealousy and greed toward *individuals* in his own little world, he contributes to the collective unconscious the negative energy which gradually builds up until it spills over, in city, state, national and international chaos.

Some of the philosophy from the Edgar Cayce readings dealing with general disturbances seems to me to be expressed in these discourses in world affairs:

And the laboring man, the daily laborer who lives by the sweat of his brow should have the consideration before the law *equal to those who direct* the lives of many! All stand as equals before the judgment bar of the Maker; and the cry of those who are oppressed goeth up to Him, ever.   3976-17

The law is universal; it applies throughout the world.
For the shoe-shiner may glorify God just as much as the king or president—and possibly more.   3521-1

Know that every other individual has as much right in the earth as you yourself have, even though in some respects he may not be as far advanced in his learning.   3633-1

During the depression of the early '30s, two Edgar Cayce readings were given which, it seems to me, speak to us now just as they did to the catastrophe of World War II which was ahead.

With the present conditions, then, that exist—these have all come to that place in the development of the human family where there must be a reckoning, a one point upon which all may agree, that out of all of this turmoil that has arisen from the social life, racial differences, the outlook upon the relationship of man to the Creative Forces or his God, and his relationships one with another, must come to some *common* basis upon which all *may* agree. You say at once, such a thing is impractical, impossible! What has caused the present conditions, not alone at home but abroad? It is that realization that was asked some thousands of years ago, "Where *is* thy brother? His blood *cries* to me from the ground!" and the other portion of the world has answered, *is* answering, "Am I my brother's keeper?" The world, *as* a world—that makes for the disruption, for the discontent—has lost its ideal. Man may not have the same *idea.* Man—*all* men—may have the *same* IDEAL!
As the Spirit of God once moved to bring peace and harmony out of chaos, so *must* the Spirit move over the earth and magnify itself in the hearts, minds and *souls* of men to bring peace, harmony and understanding, that they may dwell together in a way that will bring that peace, that harmony, that can only come with all having the *one Ideal*; not the one *idea,* but "Thou shalt love the Lord thy God with all thine heart, thy neighbor *as* thyself!" This is the whole law, this is

the whole answer to the world, to each and every soul. That is the answer to the world conditions as they exist today.

How shall this be brought about? As they each in their own respective sphere put into action that they know to be the fulfilling of that as has been from the beginning, so does the little leaven leaven the whole lump.

Man's answer to everything has been *Power*—Power of money, Power of position, Power of wealth, Power of this, that or the other. This has *never* been God's way, will never be God's way. Rather little by little, line upon line, here a little, there a little, each thinking rather of the other fellow, as that that has kept the world in the various ways of being intact— where there were ten, even, many a city, many a nation, has been kept from destruction. Though we may look upon, or feel that that which was given to Abram—as he viewed the cities of the plain and pled for the saving of same—was an allegorical story, a beautiful tale to be told children—that it might bring fear into the hearts of those that would have their *own* way— may it not come into the hearts of those now, today, wilt *thou,* thine self, make of thine *own* heart an understanding that thou must answer for thine own brother, for thine own neighbor! and who is thine neighbor? He that lives next door, or he that lives on the other side of the world? He, rather, that is in *need* of understanding! He who has faltered; he who has fallen even by the way. *He* is thine neighbor, and thou must answer for him!   3976-8, Jan. 15, 1932

A year later the admonitions were even stronger. Read these selections carefully, for they do not speak to the leaders, or the oil magnates, or the money lenders alone, but, I think, to each one of us wherever we are.

In the very nature, though, of a nation, a people, there are some fundamental principles upon which the economic and the soul life of a nation must be founded, if such a people, such a nation, is to remain true to that which is the birthright of every soul; to pursue that which will give it as an individual the right to manifest that it would worship in its Creator.

For, the first law that has been given to man from the beginning is: "Thou shalt have no other gods before me." And when man has faltered, has altered that, which has deprived others from giving expression to that birthright, that command that has come to man throughout the ages, then there arises that which creates those things that are the fruits of the evil influences that are in the earth. Such as: hate, jealousy, avarice, and the like. These make for the creating of those conditions in all walks of life for power, for position, for the love of money and that it will bring in its associations in the lives of individuals. And, as there has been just this experience in the affairs of the nation as a nation, the nation as a nation is passing through that period when each soul must turn to that thought within of what is its relation to the Creative Forces in its experience; and each soul must ask itself what it as a soul is going to do about that command that was given, and that is the privilege of every soul; to show forth that very law of love that is the birthright of every soul. For, with that command has come ever that to which mankind may expect to find himself reduced when he has forgotten that which is his *first* duty, and the second which is likened unto it; "Thou shalt love thy neighbor as thyself."

Then, this condition has been the experience in the greater portion of the whole nation, the whole world. For, that is the experience of the individual that makes for the creating in his environ, his surrounding, of that which breeds strife, that which breeds hate, that which breeds malice, that which breeds selfishness.

The next law, as man knows, is that "Like begets like." And His injunction has been: "The worlds may pass away, but my Word shall not pass away; and ye shall pay to every farthing— and, as ye do unto your neighbor, as ye purpose in your heart, so will it be measured unto you." And when conditions arise that make for distress, whether they be in body, in mind, in the economic influences in the experience of any, *sin* lieth at *thy* door. Not thine neighbor's! Blame not the other fellow. Seek first to know within self that which has prompted thee, and when thou hast set thine house in order, when thou hast made thine peace with thine own conscience (that would smite thee, if ye will look within your own heart), then may ye find the answers that will come to every soul that seeks. For, as He has given to those of old, He is the same yesterday, today and forever. Think not as to who will ascend into heaven to bring down comfort and ease to thine own aching heart, or who will go over the seas to bring that which may be of a recompense within thine own experience, but lo! ye shall find it in your own heart!

Thus has the lawgiver given, and thus has He said who has set the way to make the intercession for man: "I will not leave thee comfortless, if ye seek to do my biddings."

Many would say, "Yea, this is beautiful; yet it does not feed the hungry nor clothe those that are naked, nor make shelter for those that are cold."

Who is—Who IS—the representative of the Father in the

earth? Hath not He committed unto mankind the keeping of his brother? Hast thou answered that question that has been of old in thine experience; "Am I My Brother's Keeper?" The answer that should ring in the heart and soul of every individual is: "Know ye not that the blood of your brother crieth unto me from the ground!"

So, in the experience of those that have sent and made the conditions are greed, selfishness; that has been practiced in the minds, in the lives, in the experience of the nation. Think not any soul, "Yea, that is true for the other fellow." But it applies to Jim, to Tom, to those in ordinary walks of life, to those who have been given those powers in high places, those that have wealth about them; *they* are the oppressors; yea, look within thine own heart! Hast thou not practiced the same? For, as it has been given, "Yea, though there be only ten just men, they may save the city; they may save the nation; they may save the world," if they will but *practice* in their daily experience that which has been the command from the first: "Thou shalt love the Lord thy God with all thine heart, and thy neighbor as thyself."

This is the basis of all *spiritual* law; and to you would there be given as this:

There is no activity in the experience of man that has not its inception or purpose in a spirit of those injunctions but what *must* fail; unless it is founded in the spirit of truth.

Hence each would ask, then: "What must *I* do about it; not what shall this, that or the other ruler, other office holder, or the other individual do" but each should ask "What must *I* do about the economic conditions in which we find ourselves?"

So live each day, each hour, as to put into practice those precepts, those influences in thine own life, and in the life of all ye contact day by day. For, He hath said, "though ye wander far afield, if ye will cry unto me, if ye will ask, if ye will draw unto me, I will draw nigh unto thee; and my help, my arm is not short as man's counting of shortness, but will bring to thee speedily that which is the desire of thine heart, if it is conceived in righteousness." 　　　　3976-14, Nov. 5, 1933

There is now so much thought and talk of economic pressure that this may be unavoidable. But it seems to me that American living standards are so high in comparison with much of the world that this will bring a leveling effect rather than a chaotic upheaval. The real dangers lie, perhaps, in our congested city areas. Think for a moment of the devastation of the war years in England and Europe. The United States has not faced such strife since 1865, when the Civil War ended. Today's technological advances coupled with American help seem to have made physical and economic restoration far faster than during the latter part of the 1800s in America. In the nations of the world where relatively far more persons are directly involved in agriculture such as China, India, Africa, Russia, South America and even the middle East, the individual in many ways is better prepared to handle economic breakdown; the Chinese peasant, the African native, the villager of India depend on their own resources. If our planes stop flying and our trucks stop rolling, the breakdown in our social structure could be sudden and chaotic. Hungry mobs would be destructive! Are there enough Americans who can grow vegetables, handle simple tools, cook, can, sew, handle animals, survive? Underneath the rolls of fat, the seeming preoccupation with a lighted box in the living room, the dependence on observing rather than participating in sports, the gadget-mindedness, there is, I think, a toughness and resiliency which will enable Americans to meet the physical as well as the social stresses which they may be called upon to face.

Americans have always responded generously with help for people in need all over the world. When the Alaskan quake of 1964 occurred, there were reports of unusual feats of bravery among teenagers in helping those caught in the actual movement of land and buildings. Americans will meet the challenges of readjustments provided the difficulties are not too widespread or prolonged.

However, the combination of social upheaval (riots, mob violence, for example) brought on by the economic stress (food shortages, and/or power breakdowns) *along* with severe earth changes, may necessitate the awakening of inner strength of mind and soul, a quickening of spiritual vitality.

What would the destruction of one or more of our large commercial centers, such as Los Angeles, San Francisco or New York, do to our economy? What kind of fear patterns would sweep the nation? Could these bring a break in the moral fiber of the masses, or would the positive strengths and spiritual principles of individuals and groups spread to help sustain the balance in our society?

Chapter IV

PREPARATION FOR THE NEW AGE

Obviously we need to ask ourselves some very tough questions. It is time that we insist on some answers; not from government, state or city, not from spiritual leaders, scientists, or psychics, but from deep within ourselves. Let me share with you a few questions I have been asking myself: Do I have a spiritual ideal? Have I set mental and physical ideals which support and will help me live up to that spiritual ideal? Am I really trying daily to measure and weigh my *thoughts, words* and *actions* by those ideals? Does the very effort to live up to such standards not bring me a sense of peace and fulfillment? My answers have been, "Yes, I am trying and when the focus has been kept, there has come a better sense of rapport with my fellow man, myself, and the God I worship. Yet perhaps I have fallen away too often in these times of stress. I have returned to physical, mental and emotional activities which cannot stand observation in the light of my ideals. The results in my life have been frustrations, disappointments and feelings of separateness from my fellow men, and my concept of the Creator." I suspect that you have sensed at times these same periods of personal inadequacy.

Let us return to the admonitions in the Edgar Cayce readings which will help put this matter in perspective for us.

Tendencies in the hearts and souls of men are such that these [upheavals] may be brought about. For, as indicated through these channels oft, it is not the world, the earth, the environs about it nor the planetary influences, nor the associations or activities, that *rule* man. *Rather* does man—by *his* compliance with divine law—bring *order* out of chaos; or, by his *disregard* of the associations and laws of divine influence, bring chaos and *destructive* forces into his experience.

416-7, October 7, 1935

Our frustrations, disappointments and inadequacies then are self-induced, depending upon our degree of compliance with or disregard of Divine Law.

And again:

You must find harmony within self, you must find security within self, as has been indicated. Ye cannot create it about you until you have it within yourself.   2970-1

Edgar Cayce spells out the attitudes we need to take, the steps for each of us:

There are those forces in each individual as may respond to those creative forces in the material world, whether as respecting material things or healing, or whatnot. The *concerted* effort on the part of a group merely accentuates that as a force, or power, that may manifest in or through an individual. . .   281-5

To me he is speaking here of man's creativeness in handling matter; his capacity to awaken the Divine power of God in each of us; and, his capacity to be moved to inspired heights of expression by the beauty of the world we live in.

To some there has been given the ability to serve as prophets; some as teachers; some as ministers; some in one manner, some in another; which are spiritual gifts, and of the same source, when applied in that manner that brings service to the fellow man . . . In the association, then, as individuals . . . each, then, may serve in that way and manner as is suited to their station, position, and gifts of the Creator, through the way and manner each have applied same in the flesh.
                                              254-31

Once we accept these ideas as truth, our responsibilities become clear:

For as the time or the period draws near for these changes that come with the new order, it behooves all of those who have an ideal—as individuals, as well as groups or societies or organizations, to be practicing, applying same in their experience—and their relationships as one to another.
                                              3976-18

What is being suggested here, as I understand it, is for us to set spiritual ideals with physical and mental ideals to support the spiritual focus. Men's actions arise from attitudes, patterns of thought and habit, purposes. The thought and action which result from application of our spiritual ideals can help carry this nation through these times of crises.

How can this be done? Where can the guidance be found? *The Edgar Cayce data speaks to this point urging consistent prayer and meditation; the formation of small informal groups meeting weekly for the discussion and follow-up action on spiritual laws, plus the study and practice of meditation and prayer as a group; and finally the sharing of ideas, skills, services and talents in new community action.*

For some this means simple acts like a backyard garden and the sharing of produce know-how and encouragement; for others skills are developed, knowledge acquired and shared through groups; some may take steps to use solar heating, water and wind power for energy; some may develop knowledge and skills for working with fruit trees, bees, animals, fish; for many it is cooperation with others in energy conservation, preservation of natural resources and action for positive programs which, as they see it, will benefit mankind (international health programs would be only one example).

Practical Steps

Ideals

In 1964, Elsie Sechrist, A.R.E. lecturer and author, addressed the importance of setting ideals, in the section "Spiritual Preparation for Meditation" in her book *Meditation—Gateway to Light:* "Once more we must thoroughly examine our ideals and purposes. Surely the spiritual ideal was best expressed by Jesus who became the Christ. He did not deal with personalities, but always with principles." She later goes on to quote from the Edgar Cayce readings:

Ideals are set from spiritual purposes, spiritual aspirations, desires and there is a pattern in Him who is the way, the truth and the light, and when that pattern is set according to such judgments, we would find there is never condemning of another. Because others do not agree with thee, condemn them not. For with what judgment ye mete, it is measured to thee again. These ye find as thy greater problems in the present in relationships with others. Then analyze first thyself and thy ideals.   5255-1

38

For those activities of man or woman in the earth may not excel. . .the individual's ideal.   3407-1

The setting of ideals, spiritual, mental and physical, is emphasized and expanded in *Meditation and the Mind of Man,* by Herbert B. Puryear, Ph.D., and Mark A. Thurston, Ph.D. Chapter 6 of this book opens with what I think is an excellent statement on ideals:

"If we have set our will and mind upon spiritual growth, the first step is the setting of the spiritual ideal. In making such a conscious choice of a standard and a direction for our lives, we are providing for ourselves that which for a house is the foundation, for a ship the rudder, for a navigator is the North Star and for the mason is the plumb line. The ideal gives us a sense of stability, guidance and orientation, as well as a criterion for judgments. Without these the work of self-exploration and integration can quickly become overwhelming. For this reason the Edgar Cayce readings stress the paramount importance of setting a spiritual ideal."

There follows an important quote from an Edgar Cayce reading:

Then, the more important, the most important experience of this or any entity is to first know what is the ideal—spiritually.
                                                                                              357-13

In this chapter, Puryear and Thurston go on to stress the importance of writing down ideals. When I first read statements from the Edgar Cayce readings on this subject, I remembered a phrase, "Write these with a pencil with a large eraser." The admonition was to keep checking our decisions, thoughts, words and actions against the standards which are upgraded as we begin to refocus consciousness from self-gratification to more service-oriented purposes. For me this is well illustrated in my personal work with prayer through years of attempts to consciously relate to a Creative Power. First I prayed, God give me this or that which was desired. Then came, God make me go the way you want me to go. Next, God show me the way. And finally, gradually, is coming the simple—God use me.

Following an excellent discussion of the spiritual Ideal, Puryear and Thurston go on to develop the concepts from the readings on both mental and physical ideals. The quotes from the Edgar Cayce readings which they use focus the suggestions for the three dimensions of ideals:

. . .write the ideal *mental* attitude, as may arise from the concepts of the spiritual, [in the] relationship to self, to home, to friends, to neighbors, to thy enemies, to things, to conditions.   5091-3

For know first, the image must be in the spiritual ideal before it may become a factor in the mental self for material expression.   1440-2

On the physical ideal:

. . .the ideal material. . .Not of conditions, but what has brought, what does bring into manifestation the spiritual and mental ideals. What relationships does such bring to things, to individuals, to situations?   5091-3

Of special value for me have been the models which are presented in this chapter for writing down ideals.

By dividing the circle we can focus the spiritual ideal in mental and physical expressions toward some particular part of our lives.

Now let us take the next step by filling in the sections in the areas for mental and physical applications of the spiritual ideal in a particular life activity.

Try now putting in the center spot a word which focuses our own highest spiritual aspiration, e.g., honesty, kindness, service. Eventually we may be able to accept Jesus' statement, "I Am the Way." (John 14:6)

Let me urge you to get this book, *Meditation and the Mind of Man*, and study the chapter on ideals carefully. This is the first and essential step toward inner peace. Without the stability which comes only from within, the years ahead can only bring turmoil for you and those you love. As Puryear and Thurston say:

"Every reason that arises in our mind for not taking this manifest step may be scrutinized closely and found to be a rationalized resistance to being specific and decisive about our 'turning about.' "

Let me try to put it more bluntly. So long as we refuse to sit down and work with a spiritual ideal, reinforced by mental and physical standards for moving toward this goal, we are simply saying, "I wish to continue the rebellion against God's laws. I am not ready to try to give up my ways of gratifying myself through my power over others, my talents which glorify me, my control of material things. God, I am not sure you are there. Perhaps what I see, taste, feel, hear, smell is all there is. I'll try the way of suffering a little longer."

This chapter closes with an excellent section on ideals and affirmations. The use of affirmations, as we shall see, is a central theme in Edgar Cayce's suggestions about meditation. The final coda of this chapter is a beautiful statement, I think, for a conclusion to this brief comment on the importance of ideals.

"We are children of God, made in His image, miniature replicas of the universe, containing within us in our present finite state a pattern of wholeness. When we choose that pattern as the ideal, the motivational criterion of our lives, when we awaken it with the imaginative forces of the mind and nurture it in daily meditation and application, we begin to become that pattern. The Spirit begins to flow through us because the Spirit of love has an affinity for the pattern of love.

We begin to fulfill that for which we were created and for which we are destined; to be conformed to the image of His Son."

Prayer and Meditation

Consistent work with prayer and meditation is presented in the Edgar Cayce readings not only as essential in sustaining our movement toward a spiritual ideal, but also as a way of cleansing the blocks within our thought patterns which prevent our tapping the infinite resources of our spiritual nature. Both of these subjects, prayer and meditation, require study and application. Let me introduce this subject with part of an Edgar Cayce reading and then refer you to ways of continuing your involvement with these subjects. I am personally convinced that these disciplines must become a part of "our way of life."

In the minds of many there is little or no difference between meditation and prayer. And there are many gathered here who through their studies of various forms have very definite ideas as to meditation and prayer.

There are others who care not whether there be such things as meditation, but depend upon someone else to do their thinking, or are satisfied to allow circumstance to take its course—and hope that sometime, somewhere, conditions and circumstances will adjust themselves to such a way that the best that may be will be their lot.

Yet, to most of you, there must be something else—some desire, something that has prompted you in one manner or another to seek to be here now, that you may gather something from a word, from an act, that will either give thee hope or make thee better satisfied with thy present lot, or to *justify* thee in the course ye now pursue.

To each of you, then, we would give a word:

Ye all find yourselves confused at times, respecting from whence ye came and whither ye goeth. Ye find yourselves with bodies, with minds—not all beautiful, not all clean, not all pure in thine own sight or in thy neighbor's. And there are many who care more for the outward appearance than that which prompts the heart in its activity or in its seeking.

But, ye ask, what has this to do with meditation? What *is* meditation?

Many say that ye have no consciousness of having a soul—yet the very fact that ye hope, that ye have a desire for better things; the very fact that ye are able to be sorry or glad; indicates an activity of the mind that takes hold upon something that is not temporal in its nature—something that passeth not away with the last breath that is drawn, but takes hold upon the very source of its beginning—the *soul*—that which was made in the image of thy Maker—not thy body, no—not thy mind, but thy *soul* was in the image of thy Creator.

Then, it is the attuning of the physical and mental attributes seeking to know the relationships to the Maker. *That* is true meditation.

For ye must learn to meditate just as ye have learned to walk; to talk; to do any of the physical attributes of thy mind [with relation to] the facts, the attitudes, the conditions, the environs of thy daily surroundings.

Then there must be a conscious contact between that which is a part of the body-physical, thy body-mental, to thy soul-body, or thy superconsciousness. The names indicate that ye have given these metes and bounds, while the soul is boundless—and is represented by many means or measures or manners in the expressions in the mind of each of you.

281-41

The first course of study based on the Edgar Cayce readings was developed on the subject of meditation. This course has been given by members of the A.R.E. staff in major cities of the U.S. and Canada. It is being presented by teams of speakers in various smaller cities near major population centers. Frequent week-long conferences at A.R.E. Headquarters in Virginia Beach, Va., and elsewhere, feature this course or material from it. A bound notebook containing a study guide, the book *Meditation and the Mind of Man,* along with six taped lectures, is available for personal and group study. The *A Search for God* books of essays on spiritual laws from the Edgar Cayce readings contain chapters on meditation. These are used by some 1600 Groups throughout the U.S. and Canada. Two bound volumes of all of the Edgar Cayce data on meditation and prayer are being placed in libraries throughout the U.S. and are available to members for their personal libraries.

It is never too early or too late for one to begin daily work with prayer and meditation.

Group Study

In these times ahead we are going to need friends on the spiritual path. In a sense the small weekly Study Group has brought this phase of a spiritual community to me, and through the last forty-seven years I have seen the small *A Search for*

God groups provide nurture, encouragement and protection for many, many other seekers. The basic focus of the group effort is set forth on the first page of *The Handbook for A.R.E. Study Groups* opposite the opening chapter: ". . .choose you this day whom ye will serve. . ." (Joshua 24:15)

Q-7. Which spiritual teacher. . .would be best for me?
A-7. Why not rather turn to Him that each of these would bring to thee—thyself? Begin with those promises He hath given. Read the 14th, 15th, 16th, 17th chapters of John. *Know* they are not to someone else but to thee! And why would you use other forces when He is so nigh?

For as He has given thee, "If it were not so I would have told you."

And this means *you!*

For the Father hath promised and has given us a body, that is a temple of the living soul, which is that temple in which ye should meet Him day by day.

For as the pattern was given even in the mount of old, when ye turn to Him, He will direct thee. Why, O why, then, to any subordinate, when thy brother, thy Christ, thy Savior would speak with thee!   1299-1

It was my privilege to be a member of the first Study Group in 1932, and to help in the development of the two books, *A Search for God,* Books I and II. Through the years the group program provided the encouragement to keep going in difficult times. This help has come in five very distinct ways:

Better understanding of spiritual laws.

Encouragement in applying those laws in daily life.

Protection from the ego self.

Opportunities to serve in many ways.

Increased spiritual energy through group meditation and prayer, including physical, mental and spiritual healing.

For me, the years of group study have been a realistic approach to beginning action and movement toward a spiritual community which must be our next practical step as more stressful times occur.

Movement Toward a Spiritually Oriented Community

Most of us are not ready to sell everything we own and move to a commune or particular community. Many of man's dreams of cooperation with his fellow men have been wrecked at an international, national, state or community level when physical cooperation has been attempted before the spiritual and mental ideals have been worked through to encompass definite resolves and goals. In the face of earth changes which could bring heavy economic upheavals and breakdowns of communication, storage of quantities of food for personal survival would only bring mob violence and destruction.

What is needed, it seems to me, is the coming together of persons of like spiritual ideals. The small groups, then the area conferences, are excellent ways to begin. There must first be a willingness to share ideals, then ideas, knowledge, talents, and whatever we have in abudance, whether it be skills, vegetables or money. Don't put this down too quickly. It has been going on through the A.R.E. groups and conferences for years. Such sharing must begin in small ways and grow as the individuals grow "in spirit and in truth."

Within the last few years there has been an increasing interest on the part of A.R.E. members to think through the broadest concepts of "community": cooperative buying, sharing vegetables and produce, giving of money, time and talents to develop projects. Have you ever thought of the A.R.E. children's camp, the weeks of activities in Palestine, Texas, Asilomar in California, Seabeck in Washington, or even just a simple potluck in these terms? We must crawl before we walk, but it is perhaps time to speed up our efforts.

Conclusion

Let us close with a dream (quoted in the original *Earth Changes,* also) which Edgar Cayce had in 1936, on a train from Detroit to Virginia Beach. This followed court proceedings resulting from the family's arrest in Detroit for practicing medicine without a license. Edgar Cayce was troubled over the happening. How could the good he was trying to accomplish be so misunderstood? The dream and the reading interpreting it, follow:

"I had been born again in 2100 A.D. in Nebraska. The sea apparently covered all of the western part of the country, as the city where I lived was on the coast. The family name was a strange one. At an early age as a child I declared myself to be Edgar Cayce who had lived 200 years before.

"Scientists, men with long beards, little hair, and thick

glasses, were called in to observe me. They decided to visit the places where I said I had been born, lived and worked, in Kentucky, Alabama, New York, Michigan and Virginia. Taking me with them, the group of scientists visited these places in a long, cigar-shaped metal flying ship which moved at high speed.

"Water covered part of Alabama. Norfolk, Virginia, had become an immense seaport. New York had been destroyed either by war or an earthquake and was being rebuilt. Industries were scattered over the countryside. Most of the houses were of glass.

"Many records of my work as Edgar Cayce were discovered and collected. The group returned to Nebraska taking the records with them to study."

Reading:

These experiences, as has oft been indicated, come to the body in those manners in which there may be help, strength, for periods when doubt or fear may have arisen. As in this experience, there were about the entity those influences which appeared to make for such a record of confusion as to appear to the material or mental-minded as a doubting or fearing of those sources that made for the periods through which the entity was passing in that particular period.

And the vision was that there might be strength, there might be an understanding that though the moment may appear as dark, though there may be periods of the misinterpreting of purposes, even *these* will be turned into that which will be the very proof itself in the experiences of the entity and those whom the entity might, whom the entity would in its experience through the earth plane, help; and those to whom the entity might give hope and understanding.

This then is the interpretation. As has been given, "Fear not." Keep the faith; for those that be with thee are greater than those that would hinder. Though the very heavens fall, though the earth shall be changed, though the heavens shall pass, the promises in Him are sure and will stand—as in that day—as the proof of thy activity in the lives and hearts of thy fellow man.

For indeed and in truth ye know, "As ye do it unto thy fellow man, ye do it unto thy God, to thyself." For *self* effaced, God may indeed glorify thee and make thee *stand* as one that is called for a purpose in the dealings, the relationships with thy fellow man.

Be not unmindful that He is nigh unto thee in every trial, in every temptation, and hath not willed that thou shouldst perish.

Make thy will then one with His. Be not afraid.

That is the interpretation. That the periods from the material angle as visioned are to come to pass matters not to the soul, but do thy duty *today! Tomorrow* will care for itself.

These changes in the earth will come to pass, for the time and times and half times are at an end, and there begin those periods for the readjustments. For how hath He given? "The righteous shall inherit the earth."

Hast thou, my brethren, a heritage in the earth?

294-185, June 30, 1936

Editor's Note: For more information on Study Groups and/or locating Groups meeting in your area, please write to the Study Group Dept., P.O. Box 595, Virginia Beach, VA 23451. The books mentioned in this chapter can be ordered through the A.R.E. Press at the above address.

RESOURCES BIBLIOGRAPHY

Community
Hawken, Paul. *The Magic of Findhorn*. New York: Harper and Row, 1975.

Kriyananda, Swami. *Cooperative Communities—How to Start Them and Why*. Nevada City, Ca., Ananda Publications, 1972.

Education and Games
The Findhorn Foundation, ed. *Festivals in the New Age*. The Park, Forres, Moray, Scotland: Findhorn Publications, 1975.

Hills, Christopher. *Exploring Inner Space*. Awareness Games for All Ages. Boulder Creek, Ca.; University of the Trees Press, 1978.

James, Walene. *Handbook for Educating in the New Age*. Based on the Edgar Cayce Readings. Virginia Beach, Va.: A.R.E. Press, 1977.

Fluegelman, Andrew, ed. *The New Games Book*. Garden City, N.Y.: Dolphin/Doubleday, 1976.

Gardening and Foods
Angier, Bradford. *Field Guide to Edible Wild Plants*. Harrisburg, Pa.: Stackpole Books, 1974.

Harris, Ben Charles. *Eat the Weeds*. Barre, Mass.: Barre Publications, 1971.

Johnson, Mary. *Tub Farming*. Charlotte, Vt.: Garden Way Publications, 1978.

Mead, Gretchen, and Thurber, Nancy. *Home Storage of Vegetables and Fruits*. Charlotte, Vt.: Garden Way Publications, 1976.

Raymond, Dick. *Down to Earth Gardening Know-How*. Edited by Charles Cook. Charlotte, Vt.: Garden Way Publications, 1979.

How to Dry Fruits and Vegetables at Home, by the Editors of *Farm Journal*. Garden City, N.J.: Doubleday & Co., 1979.

Healing and Health
Gaskin, Ina May. *Spiritual Midwifery*. Summertown, Pa.: The Book Publishing Co., 1978.

Joy, W. Brugh. *Joy's Way*. Los Angeles, Ca.: J.B. Tarcher, 1978.

Pelletier, Kenneth R. *Mind as Healer, Mind as Slayer*. New York: Dell Publishing Co., 1977.

Puryear, Meredith Ann. *Healing Through Meditation and Prayer*. Based on the Edgar Cayce Readings. Virginia Beach, Va.: A.R.E. Press, 1978.

Reilly, Harold J. and Brod, Ruth Hagy. *The Edgar Cayce Handbook for Health through Drugless Therapy*. New York: Macmillan Publishing Co., 1975.

Weiner, Michael. *Earth Medicine—Earth Foods*. London: Collier MacMillan Publishing Co., 1978.

New Age Philosophy
Ballard, Juliet Brooke. *The Hidden Laws of Earth*. Based on the Edgar Cayce Readings. Virginia Beach, Va.: A.R.E. Press, 1979.
Fromm, Eric. *The Revolution of Hope; Toward a Humanized Technology*. New York: Bantam, 1968.
Fuller, R. Buckminster. *Utopia or Oblivion: The Prospects for Humanity*. New York: Bantam, 1969.
Sande, Nathaniel. *Mindstyles/Lifestyles: A Comprehensive Overview of Today's Life-Changing Philosophies*. Los Angeles: Price/Stern/Sloan Publishers, 1976.
Pearce, Joseph Chilton. *The Crack in the Cosmic Egg: Challenging Constructs of Mind and Reality*. New York: Julian, 1971.
Rudhyar, Dane. *The Planetarization of Consciousness: From the Individual to the Whole*. New York: Harper and Row, 1972.
Spangler, David. *Relationship and Identity*. Forres, Scotland: Findhorn Publications, 1977.
Spangler, David. *The Laws of Manifestation*. Marina Del Rey, Ca.: DeVorss and Co., 1978.
Thompson, William Irwin. *Darkness and Scattered Light*. Four Talks of the Future. New York: Doubleday, 1978.

New Age Technology
Carr, Donald. *Energy and the Earth Machine*. Norton Press, 1976.
Harper, Peter; Boyle, Godfrey; editors of *Undercurrents;* eds. *Radical Technology*. New York: Random House, 1976.
Havens, David. *The Woodburner's Handbook*. Rekindling an Old Romance. Brunswick, Me.: Harpswell Press, 1973.
Mayria, Edward. *The Passive Solar Energy Book*. A Complete Guide to Passive Solar Home, Greenhouse and Building Design. Emmaus, Pa.: Rodale Press, 1979.
Watson, Donald. *Designing and Building a Solar House: Your Place in the Sun*. Charlotte, Vt.: Garden Way Publications, 1977.

Reference Guides
Carnahan, Don. *Guide to Alternative Periodicals*. St. Petersburg Beach, Fla.: Sunspark Press, 1977.
Khalsa, Parmatma Singh. *Spiritual Communities Guide,* #4, 1979. The New Consciousness Sourcebook. San Rafael, Ca.: Spiritual Communities Publishers/NAM, 1979.

Recommended Periodicals
Alternatives: Newmarket, Va.
The Mother Earth News: Hendersonville, N.C.
Resurgence: Journal of the Fourth World: Devon, England.

Part II

Earth Changes:
Past—Present—Future

by a Geologist

Preface

This material is the visible manifestation of one individual's encounter with the Edgar Cayce readings. It relates the findings and activities of a person who sought literal verification of geological information in the psychic discourses. During the course of his research, between 1957 and 1970, the author gradually became aware of several aspects of the readings that have yet to be adequately explored. Among these are: (1) the various sources of psychic information that may be tapped, (2) the conditioning of the psychic data transmitted by the motives of those seeking the information, and (3) the use of allegory in the readings.

The A.R.E. Press discontinued publication of *Earth Changes* in 1971. The geological information presented was largely out of date. Furthermore, various crustal movements predicted by some of the readings, including the emergence of the sea-floor in the Bahamas area in 1968 or 1969, did not occur. The Edgar Cayce Foundation has decided to have the 1968 version of *Earth Changes* reprinted because of the significant role that it played in motivating a scientific approach to analysis of the readings. Although the scientific approach suffers from the limitations of any defined method of investigation, it does provide useful counterpoint to the uncritical-acceptance mode of analysis often displayed by psychical researchers. The Foundation hopes that reprinting this work will encourage other scientists to examine readings peculiar to their disciplines.

*A Geologist**

---

*The author is a professional geologist, holding the S.B., S.M., and Ph.D. degrees in his field. He has made numerous original investigations of natural phenomena and has authored a number of research papers for scientific journals. His name is withheld at his request.

Abstract

Study of approximately fifty Edgar Cayce readings that describe past geologic events indicates that the information given in the readings is internally logical and consistent. Twenty of these readings, which describe events of earth history that occurred as early as Pliocene time (10,000,000 B.C.), are presented. The readings are compared to recent scientific information. Only a few of the statements in the twenty readings agree closely with current scientific *facts;* a number of them stand in contrast to present scientific *concepts* of earth history.

Most of the readings on prehistorical subjects were given in the 1920s and 1930s, and all were on file before 1945 when Cayce died. It is thus clear that the majority of the psychic statements antedate nearly all of the striking discoveries recently made by such youthful fields of scientific endeavor as deep-sea research, paleomagnetic research, and research on the absolute age of geologic materials. Whereas the results of recent research sometimes modify, or even overthrow, important *concepts* of geology, they often have the opposite effect, in relation to the psychic readings, in that they tend to render them the more probable.

Fifteen psychic readings are presented in this paper that treat current or future geologic events for the period from 1958 to 2001 A.D. The many catastrophic events that are predicted for this period are out of harmony with the standard geological *concept* of uniformitarianism, or gradual change. It is of interest, however, that certain events predicted in the readings, for the period of 1926 to 1958, occurred as prophesied. Examples are an earthquake in California on October 22, 1926; violent wind storms on the 15th and 20th of October, 1926; and the general location of strong earthquakes in California between 1926 and 1950.

It is possible that certain geological events, of the sort which the readings predicted would precede the large-scale earth changes, are actually coming about.

Introduction

General Statement

Many of the lay and professional people who have studied the Edgar Cayce psychic readings have expressed an interest in knowing what sort of correspondence there might be between the geological and related material found in the readings and concepts of earth history which have been formed through scientific research. This booklet has been prepared for the purpose of briefly reviewing the correspondence that exists between the Edgar Cayce psychic data and scientific interpretations of earth changes during periods paralleled by the readings.[1]

The Psychic Data

The psychic data cited in this study are available on open file at the A.R.E. Library/Conference Center in Virginia Beach, Virginia. The information cited herein consists of short quotes from about 40 readings that deal with geological or related historical material; in all, there are available some 14,256 transcripts of "readings" that were given through Mr. Cayce during a period of about 40 years. As the cross-indexing of readings is an ongoing process, it may be that a few of them will be found to contain additional data of the sort included in this study. A few of the quotations in this article may be seen in context only at the Edgar Cayce Foundation; many of them, however, are available in publications of one form or another from the A.R.E. Press.

The Scientific Data

The scientific data that are cited in this study are essentially short quotes or statements from the scientific literature—

---

1. First published January 12, 1959; revised April, 1961. Addendum, March, 1968.

statements which involve, primarily, *facts*. Scientific *concepts* have been cited in only a few instances (where they are relatively inseparable from facts). In this way the reader may make comparisons between the psychic and scientific information in a simple manner and draw his own conclusions. Attempts to fit the psychic data into this or that scientific theory have been carefully avoided as has also any attempt to develop new theories based upon these data.

Text Format

Excerpts from the readings appear in bold and are arranged chronologically according to the periods of earth history which they cover (past, present, and future included). The approximate period of time covered by a given excerpt is indicated by the italicized heading above each reading. Over half of the dates given are "before the present" (B.P.); that is, before 1958. The corresponding B.C. date is usually given in parentheses. All A.D. dates are listed as such. A number and date appear at the end of each reading and indicate the case number (or file number) and date when the reading itself was given. All editorial notes made in the readings are enclosed in brackets. Scientific data that bear upon the period of time covered by a reading appear in standard type just below the reading excerpt.

The very first reading which follows carries typical introductory passages—these have been omitted from the other readings that are cited.

COMPARISONS OF THE PSYCHIC AND SCIENTIFIC DATA

10,500,000 B.P.

This psychic reading was given by Edgar Cayce at his office, 332 Grafton Avenue, Dayton, Ohio, May 28, 1925, in accordance with request made by self—Edgar Cayce, at 11:30 A.M., D.S.T. Present: Edgar Cayce; Gertrude Cayce (conductor); Gladys Davis (stenographer).

Mrs. Cayce: You will have before you the psychic work of Edgar Cayce, present in this room, especially that phase pertaining to life readings and former appearances of individuals in the earth's plane. In several readings there has been given information concerning the second ruler in Egypt who gave the first laws concerning man's relation to the Higher Forces. You will give me an outline of this teaching and how same was given to the people.

Mr. Cayce: Yes, we have the work here and that phase concerning the indwelling in the earth's plane of those who first gave laws concerning indwelling of Higher Forces in man. In giving such in an understandable manner to man of today, [it is] necessary that the conditions of the earth's surface and the position of man in the earth's plane be understood, for the change has come often since this period, era, age of man's earthly indwelling, for then at that period only the lands now known as the Sahara and the Nile region appeared on the now African shores; that in Tibet, Mongolia, Caucasia and Norway [appeared] in Asia and Europe; that in the southern cordilleras and Peru in the southwestern hemisphere and the plane of now [present] Utah, Arizona, Mexico of the northwestern hemisphere, and the spheres were then in the latitudes much as are presented at the present time.

... man's indwelling was then in the Sahara and the upper Nile regions, the waters then entering the now Atlantic from the Nile region rather than flowing northward. The waters in the Tibet and Caucasian entering the North Sea; those in the cordilleras entering the Pacific; those in the plateau entering the Northern Seas.

When the earth brought forth the seed in her season, and man came in the earth plane as the lord of that in that sphere, man appeared in five places then at once—the five senses, the five reasons, the five spheres, the five developments, the five nations.   5748-1, May 28, 1925

Now, as we see, as given, how and what the classifications were of the physical in the earth's plane at that period, the numbers of human souls then in the earth plane at that period, the numbers of human souls then in the earth plane being a hundred and thirty and three million [133,000,000] souls. The beginning then of the understanding of laws as applied from man's viewpoint being in this second rule in the country now Egypt. The rule covering the period of a hundred and ninety and nine [199] years, and the entity giving the chance to the peoples for the study, being in the twenty and eighth [28th] year, when he began to gather the peoples together for this and surrounding himself with those of that land and of the various lands wherein the human life dwelled at that period. The numbers of people that came together for the purpose then numbering some forty and four [44].

The Courts as were made were in the tents and the caves of the dwellers of the then chosen priest from the Arabian or Tibetan country, who came as one among those, to assist with the astrologer and the soothsayers of the desert of now the eastern and western worlds, and with this the conclave was held for many, many moons. The period in the world's existence from the present time being ten and one-half million [10,500,000] years, and [in] the changes that have come in the earth's plane many have risen in the lands. Many lands have disappeared, many have appeared and disappeared again and again during these periods, gradually changing as the condition became to the relative position of the earth with the other spheres through which man passes in this solar system.
                                    5748-2, May 28, 1925

Miocene sediments have recently been dated at approximately 12,000,000 years in age. (Lipson, 1958, p. 137) A date of 10,500,000 years would roughly mark the Miocene-Pliocene boundary on the geologic time scale.[2] Referring to Dunbar (1949, fig. 253C) it can be seen that about Miocene-

2. The particular time scale used here would start with earliest Pliocene at 10,500,000 B.P. and would have the Pliocene (Tertiary) end about 600,000 B.P. The Pleistocene (Quaternary) would begin, therefore, about 600,000 B.P. and the first glaciation would be about 280,000 B.P. (Cf. Emiliani, 1955)

Pliocene time North America had very nearly its present configuration, with the exception of some submergence of the coastal plains (especially the Gulf Coastal plain where a remnant of the Mississippi Valley embayment persisted). Land-sea relationships of most of the rest of the world during Miocene-Pliocene time have yet to be completely worked out.

Neither the original locations of the first "human beings" nor the date of their appearance has been established by scientific research and, indeed, some workers have concluded that "so far science has thrown no light on the origin of man." (Dewar, 1954) Fossil fragments have been found in Tuscany, Italy, however, which indicate that human-like creatures (hominids) lived in the area as early as "the lower Pliocene or upper Miocene. . ." (de Terra, 1956, p. 1284); that is, some 10 to 11 million years ago.

10,000,000 B.P.

Q-5. Did the appearance of what became the five races occur simultaneously?
A-5. Occurred at once.
Q-6. Describe the earth's surface at the period of the appearance of the five projections.
A-6. This has been given. In the first or that known as the beginning, or in the Caucasians and Carpathian, or the Garden of Eden, in that land which lies now much in the desert, yet much in mountain and much in the rolling lands there. The extreme northern portions were then the southern portions, or the polar regions were then turned to where they occupied more of the tropical and semi-tropical regions; hence it would be hard to discern or disseminate the change. The Nile entered into the Atlantic Ocean. What is now the Sahara was an inhabited land and very fertile. What is now the central portion of the country, or the Mississippi basin, was then all in the ocean; only the plateau was existent, or the regions that are now portions of Nevada, Utah, and Arizona formed the greater part of what we know as the United States. That [land?] along the Atlantic [sea]board formed the outer portion then, or the lowlands of Atlantis. The Andean or the Pacific coast of South America occupied then the extreme western portion of Lemuria. The Urals and the northern regions of same were turned into a tropical land. The desert in the Mongolian land was then the fertile portion. This may enable you to form *some* concept of the status of the earth's representations at that time! The oceans were then turned

about; they no longer bear their names, yet from whence obtained they their names? What is the legend, even, as to their names?   364-13, November 17, 1932

. . . in the ruins as are found that have arisen, in the mounds and caves in the northwestern portion of New Mexico, may be seen some of the drawings the entity then made. Some ten million years ago.   2665-2, July 17, 1925

"Ten million years ago"—the Basin and Range Province (includes northwest New Mexico) had developed its modern aspect. (Dunbar, 1949, fig. 253C) "Mounds and caves" as old as 10,000,000 years could be preserved, therefore, until the present day.

230,000-30,000 B.P.

. . . the variations [in Atlantis], as we find, extend over a period of some two hundred thousand (200,000) years—that is, light years, as known in the present—and that there were *many* changes in the surface of what is now called the earth. In the first or greater portion, we find that *now* known as the southern portions of South America and the Arctic or North Arctic regions, while those in what is *now* as Siberia—or that as of Hudson Bay—was rather in the region of the tropics, or the position now occupied by near what would be as the same *line* would run, of the southern Pacific, or central Pacific regions—and about the same way. Then we find, with this change that came first in that portion, when the first of those peoples used that as prepared *for* the changes in the earth, we stood near the same position as the earth occupies in the present—as to Capricorn, or the equator, or the poles. Then, with that portion, *then* the South Pacific, or Lemuria [?] began its disappearance—even before Atlantis . . .
                                364-4, February 16, 1932

Internal consistency of psychic statements: The key word is *western.* The Pacific coast of South America occupied the extreme *western* portion of Lemuria. By rotating a globe so that the southern portions of South America, the Arctic or north Arctic regions, Siberia, and Hudson Bay occupy positions in the southern and central Pacific regions, one can see that the present Pacific coast of South America does occupy "the extreme western [more nearly northwestern] portion" of a reconstructed continent called "Lemuria." Other conditions in the psychic statement appear satisfied by this rotation. The Urals "and the northern regions of same" are "turned into a tropical land." "The desert in the Mongolian land" (the Gobi desert) becomes "the fertile portion" because the prevailing winds reaching the area are moisture-carrying. These winds (from the "west") would derive their moisture from the (now) southwestern Pacific—the (then) northeastern south Pacific. (This speculation assumes that the oceanic circulation off the west coast of Mongolia was of the type conducive to development of moisture-carrying winds, just as the present Gulf Stream is responsible for moisture in the air mass moving across northern Europe of today.)

Location of the North and South Poles: According to the foregoing psychic statement, the geographic position of the North Pole would be in the vicinity of 15° south latitude and 40° east longitude or, very roughly, Mozambique, Mozambique. The geographic South Pole would be in the vicinity of 15° north latitude and 140° west longitude or, roughly, some 1,300 miles east-southeast of the Hawaiian Islands.

It would be well to review briefly current thought on polar displacement. Studies of remanent magnetization in rocks of various ages, by Runcorn (1956 *a*, 1956 *b*) and by many others, indicate that polar "wandering" throughout geologic time is a strong probability. Directions of the earth's magnetic field have been determined for a large range of geologic time. The assumption made is that the geomagnetic field has nearly always been symmetrical about the earth's axis of rotation, and of dipole character. The discovery of a reversal in the earth's magnetic field near the Pliocene-Pleistocene geologic time boundary (Opdyke and Runcorn, 1956) has been interpreted as a change in the polarity of the magnetic field (*Ibid.*, p. 1127) rather than an 180° change in the poles of the axis of the earth's rotation. In certain periods reversals of the geomagnetic field may have been very frequent and in others rather rare. (Runcorn, 1956 *b*, p. 315) Creer (1958, p. 101) has recently reported "occasional, yet well-defined directions of magnetization differing up to 60° from the mean" for rocks some 250 million years old and suggests that a substantial amount of polar wandering must have occurred during those (Carboniferous) times.

Momose (1958, table 1) presents evidence, from a study of the residual magnetism of Japanese volcanic rocks and sediments, that the direction of the centered geomagnetic dipole was in the vicinity of 15° south latitude and 23° east longitude at one period during late Pliocene time. He does not go so far, however, as to say that this position of the geomagnetic North Pole would correspond to the North Pole of the earth's rotational axis; rather, he merely states (p. 12): ". . . as far as the writer's examination goes, it should be stressed that the direction of the earth's magnetic dipole axis in Pliocene age would have shifted from the North Polar region, continuously southward to the South Polar region." It should be emphasized here, however, that if this particular evidence of Momose's—of a north magnetic pole in the vicinity of Mozambique during the late Pliocene—were lacking, the case for the rotation of the globe suggested by the psychic data would be very weak indeed. Of further importance is the following excerpt which involved a question about the original locations of the five races of man.

Q-7. Are the following the correct places? Atlantean, the red [race]?

A-7. Atlantean and American, the red race.

Q-8. Upper Africa for the black?

A-8. Or what would be known now as the more western portion of upper Egypt for the black. You see, with the changes—when there came the uprisings in the Atlantean land, and the sojourning southward—with the turning of the axis, the white and yellow races came more into that portion of Egypt, India, Persia and Arabia. 364-13, November 17, 1932

The "turning of the axis" is mentioned, and it is significant that Momose found evidence for the *continuous* shift of the *geomagnetic-dipole* axis during the same general period covered by the reading. It is perhaps not too dangerous to at least speculate that the earth's rotational axis followed closely the movements of the geomagnetic-dipole axis.

Reference to "the Arctic or North Arctic regions" being "in the region of the tropics": According to the rotation of the globe just described, Alaska would have been in the region of the tropics from at least 230,000 B.P. to perhaps 52,000 B.P. (Whether or not the North Pole was migrating by short steps toward its present position is not indicated.) Gidley (1913, p. 1) found remains of a camel, elephant, and other animals in Alaska and he believed that these fossils added "proof in support of the supposition that milder climatic conditions prevailed in Alaska during probably the greater part of the Pleistocene period."

It is also true that by this rotation Australia would have been at the equator. Ewing and Donn (1958, p. 1162) cite Benson (1921) as indicating that "during the Pleistocene, fauna with tropical affinities inhabited Australia." Finally, Antarctica would have been located from approximately 10° to 40° north of the equator, according to the position of the poles described in the psychic statement. The present area of the Ross Ice Shelf and Ross Sea would have been located nearly on the equator. In a study of cores taken from the bottom of the Ross Sea, however, Hough (1950, pp. 257-259) found evidence of glacial activity on the Antarctic continent during much of the time between 230,000 B.P. and 52,000 B.P. Materials from the cores in question were dated by the ionium[3] method. It would be unlikely that any of the Antarctic continent would have been glaciated if it were in such an equatorial position unless a high mountain range, which was capable of supporting glaciers, existed near the Ross Sea.

Reference to "Atlantis": A reference is made to the continent of Atlantis whose lowlands paralleled the present "Atlantic [sea]board." Geological evidence that might support such a reconstruction seems to be found in Drake, and others (1957, p. 1718), who describe geosynclines off the east coast of North America north of Cape Hatteras. The great volume and character of sediments encountered in the more seaward of the synclinal flexures (which parallel the coast) is suggestive of a continental source to the east, in the mid-Atlantic.

Two articles which have important bearing on the hypothetical continent of Atlantis stand in apparent opposition to one another. Kolbe (1957) studied deep-sea core materials taken from a depth of about two miles at a point on part of the mid-Atlantic submarine ridge. He reported finds of exclusively fresh-water plants (diatoms) in portions of the sedimentary materials and concluded, in part, that this constituted evidence that this part of the mid-Atlantic submarine ridge was once above sea level. Rigby and Burckle (1958) have suggested an alternative explanation (turbidity-

---

3. "Uranium in sea water decays to thorium (ionium) which is precipitated on the bottom of the ocean. . .Thorium has a half life of 80,000 years and its separation from its parent offers a potential method of age measurement." (Pettersson, 1954, p. 329) "Although the simple radium-thorium method may be invalid, there are still some indirect methods for realizing the same purpose. . ." (*Ibid.,* p. 330); ". . .The method is liable to error arising from a possible change in the rate of thorium precipitation." (*Ibid.,* p. 331)

current emplacement) for Kolbe's findings, but Kolbe (1958) has defended his original hypothesis.

Emiliani (1958) recently studied a deep-sea core which was taken in water over 2.5 miles deep at the following mid-north Atlantic location: 34° 57′ N and 44°16′ W (site A, figure 1). The location of this core is toward the center of the continent of Atlantis which is described in the reading above and in several subsequent readings. Emiliani (*ibid.*, p. 266) indicates that the

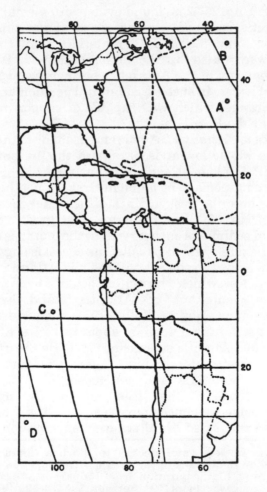

Figure 1—Map showing sites of deep sea cores A, B, C, D, mentioned in text. Dashed line represents possible outline of western boundary of "Atlantis" prior to first destruction described in readings. [Compare this outline with Heezen and Tharp (1958).]

upper half or more of the core he studied appears "to present an undisturbed record" [of sedimentation] which, according to his methods of analysis, indicates that the locality of the core in question was ocean bottom for the last 280,000 and more years. No radiocarbon[4] or ionium dates for materials in this core have been published.

Evidence which is potentially even more damaging to the theory of Atlantis than the results of Emiliani's study was incorporated in a book of speculations entitled *Earth's Shifting Crust,* by C.H. Hapgood (1958). On page 294 and in figure 9 the author discusses a deep-sea core which was taken in the mid-north Atlantic, approximately 1300 kilometers east of St. Johns, Newfoundland, and in the latitude of Nova Scotia (site B, figure 1). *Materials in the core have been dated by the ionium method and the dates obtained indicate that the core in question has been ocean bottom for the last 72,500 years.*

The precise outlines of the continent of Atlantis were never given in a Cayce reading, but it may be asking too much to assume that this core locality in the mid-north Atlantic was just off the coast of hypothetical Atlantis. Granted that this *were* true, however, some interesting comparisons could be made between the Atlantis readings and the log of this core. The zone of warm-water deposits (water decidedly warmer than present) toward the base of this core, for instance, could be correlated with a shift in the position of the North Pole as described in the above readings. The equator at this time (according to the readings) might have been closer to the present north Atlantic. During the changing of the poles (see reading 5249-1, p. 69), the resulting volcanism could have produced the zone of volcanic-glass shards (dated at about 51,400 to 55,400 B.P.) in this core and the zone of glacial-marine deposits above the volcanic material would correspond with the

---

4. "In 1946, W.F. Libby published the conception of the neutrons released by the cosmic radiation being bound to transform the atmospheric nitrogen atoms into radioactive carbon of the same atomic weight; i.e., C^{14}. In 1947, W.F. Libby and his co-workers succeeded in proving the existence of natural radiocarbon (C^{14}) by experiment; during the next years they developed the radiocarbon dating method and published the first C^{14} dates in 1950. Improved techniques devised in many laboratories during the following six years have proved the radiocarbon method to be of eminent importance for the late quaternary geology, for paleontology, and prehistoric archaeology. A presumption must be stressed; unobjectionable samples for radiocarbon dating have to be collected..." (Gross, 1957, p. 141)

glaciation indicated after polar displacement (reading 5249-1, p. 69).

Mellis (1958), in a study of the genesis of the deep-sea sands in the Atlantic Ocean, indicates that the sands of the Romanche Deep probably originated from the weathering of parts of the mid-Atlantic ridge that once projected above the sea's surface. A report in the *Military Engineer* (Anon., 1959, p. 403) states: ". . . during hydrographic surveys by the U.S. Coast and Geodetic Survey, sinkholes as large as half a mile in diameter and 500 feet deep were discovered in the Straits of Florida 14 miles offshore from the Florida Keys where the ocean bottom is 900 feet deep. They are presumed to have been freshwater lakes in an area which subsided." This last finding is of interest with regard to the following fragment of a reading that indicates that a part of lost Atlantis may be found off Bimini, beneath the Gulf Stream; that is, "in the Straits of Florida."

The position as the continent Atlantis occupied, is that as between the Gulf of Mexico on the one hand—and the Mediterranean upon the other. Evidences of this lost civilization are to be found in the Pyrenees and Morocco on the one hand, British Honduras, Yucatan and America upon the other. There are some protruding portions within this that must have at one time or another been a portion of this great continent. The British West Indies or the Bahamas, and a portion of same that may be seen in the present—if the geological survey would be made in some of these—especially, or notably, in Bimini and in the Gulf Stream through this vicinity, these may be even yet determined.

364-3, February 16, 1932

A series of readings given on the islands of Bimini, that lie roughly 60 miles east of Miami, are of considerable interest. The first in the series begins:

Dr. H.: You will give a reading on Bimini Island . . . and tell us whether there is oil on this island in sufficient quantities to insure profit. If so, give us the log of the formations, etc. . .

Mr. Cayce: Yes, we have the land known as Bimini, in the Atlantic Ocean. In the formation of the land, we find this of the nature that would make the oil production very low, for this is of coral structure in the greater part, but, this is the highest portion left above the waves of a once great continent, upon which the civilization as now exists in the world's history

found much of that as would be used as means for attaining that civilization.			996-1, August 14, 1926

The last of the readings in this series (996-12) states that the minerals "gold, spar, and icthyolite [?]" will be found there at depth, as well as remains "of the first highest civilization that will be uncovered in some of the adjacent lands to the west and south of the isles."

Q-3. How deep in the ground will that [the minerals and archaeological remains] be found?
A-3. . . . these will be found in the twelve to fifteen (12 to 15) foot levels [below sea level, in the context of the entire reading]. The *vein*, as workable, would be found extending in the northeast southwest direction.			996-12

This last depth value is of interest in view of a radioactive carbon date of 4370 years B.P. (Broecker and Kulp, 1957, p. 1328) for a sample of mangrove peat encountered at a depth of 9 feet below mean low water in a core boring on Bimini. The date suggests that any materials encountered in the "twelve to fifteen foot levels" would be only a few thousand years older than about 4370 years, and might possibly be of the order of 10,100 years or slightly more, the date given for the final destruction of Atlantis.

References to "Lemuria": There are a few references to a "Lemurian" continent in the Cayce readings. This continent would have been located in the southeastern Pacific Ocean of the present day and one coast would have coincided with the present west coast of South America. The evidence for repeated elevations and founderings of continental-sized blocks of the earth's crust is in no way contrary to modern concepts of earth history. (Cf. Umbgrove, 1947, pp. 30 and 241) Research on this southeastern Pacific area of the earth's crust is scanty, however. A scientific reference which treats Pacific-basin crustal structures is authored by Menard and Fisher (1958). It shows (*ibid.*, fig. 8) a deep trench off part of the Andean coast of South America. At least one other deep submarine trench, however, shows evidence of once being part of a continent. (Umbgrove, 1947, p. 38) In a later paper, Menard (1958) states: "The southern part of the east Pacific Rise is 2000 km. wide and 2 km. high—one of the largest oceanic rises in the world... Observations do not rule out the possibility that broad rises may be temporary features which are elevated and then subside."

Hough (1953) studied two Pacific bottom cores from the vicinity of hypothetical "Lemuria" (sites C and D, figure 1). Core one was taken at 8°56' S and 92°5' W from a depth of 12,900 feet; core two was taken at 32°21' S and 105°55' W from a depth of 11,880 feet. (*Ibid.*, 1953, p. 252) The sediments in both cores are representative of normal marine, deep-sea sedimentation. Both cores were dated by the ionium method. The bottom of core one was estimated to be 990,000 years in age. The bottom of core two was estimated at 1,231,000 years in age. (*Ibid.*, 1953, p. 252) Thus, assuming the reliability of the ionium method of dating, proper interpretation of the core materials, and *assuming* that cores were taken in places where land bodies are alleged to have been, no continent of Lemuria, as described in the readings, could have been in existence between 230,000 and 30,000 B.P. at these localities.

An interesting sidelight on the reliability of the ionium method of age-determination is found in Goldberg and Koide (1958, p. 1003): "Surface values of the [ionium-thorium] ratio were not constant over the eastern Pacific Ocean. This observation may result from differences in thorium isotope concentrations in near bottom waters which furnish these isotopes to sediments. A dramatic drop in the Io/Th ratio, corresponding to nearly 2 half-lives of ionium over a few centimeters' distance, is observed in the Down-wind core [lat. 42°02' S., long. 98°01' W]. Such a change has been observed in but one other core, also from these southerly latitudes."

A report in *The New York Times* of April 12, 1959, describes discovery of a vast layer of "clean white ash" on the Pacific Ocean floor a few hundred miles from Central and South America, extending 750 miles to the north and 825 miles to the south of the equator. Initial speculations are that it represents "widespread volcanic action" of falling debris from "a collision of heavenly bodies in outer space." Anders and Limber (1959) believe the ash to be of terrestrial, rather than extraterrestrial, origin. At any rate, the ash layer is believed "to record a notable event in the earth's history." One asks, could this event be in some way related to "Lemuria's" death?

52,680 B.P. (50,772 B.C.)

A question was asked in reference to a previous reading that had described a meeting of world leaders that was held for the purpose of discussing destruction of "the enormous animals which overran the earth":

Q-14. What was the date B.C. of this gathering?
A-14. 50,772.   262-39, February 21, 1933

Another reading on this same subject:

The entity then was among those who were of that group who gathered to rid the earth of the enormous animals which overran the earth, but ice, the entity found, nature, God, changed the poles and the animals were destroyed, though man attempted it in that activity of the meetings.
                                        5249-1, June 12, 1944

Reference to "enormous animals which overran the earth": "Throughout the Pleistocene epoch [approximately 600,000 to 11,000 B.P.] North America and Europe were both inhabited by great game animals fully as varied and impressive as those of modern East Africa." (Dunbar, 1949, p. 489) A partial list includes elephants, "four species, two of which exceeded modern elephants in size. The tall rangy imperial mammoth of the southern Great Plains stood 14 feet high at the shoulders. Another species (*Mammuthus arizonae*) was at home in the basins of Arizona and Nevada. Throughout the forests mastodons (*Mammut americanus*) browsed in great herds." (*Ibid.*, 1949, pp. 489-490; fig. 319) Horses abounded, "one fully equaled the greatest modern draught horse." (*Ibid.*, p. 490) There were seven species of buffaloes "and one of these (*Bison latifrons*) was a colossal beast with a horn-spread of fully 6 feet." (*Ibid.*, p. 490; fig. 319) A great cat (*Felis atrox*) and the great wolf (*Canis dirus*) "exceeded in size any modern American canines." (*Ibid.*, p. 491) The musk ox, woolly rhinoceros, great groundsloth, bear, wild pig, camel, and giant beaver also abounded. "In Europe, the Pleistocene fauna of the warm interglacial ages [the Riss-Wurm interglacial was terminated about 52,000 B.P. (cf. Emiliani, 1955; fig. 15)] included most of the types of great game animals now found in Africa." (*Ibid.*, p. 492)
Reference to the changing of the poles: An hypothesis involving movements of the north geographic pole from a position outside the Arctic Ocean to its present position inside this ocean has been advanced recently (Ewing and Donn, 1958; p. 1159) to explain the initiation of an ice age. Studies of deep-

sea sediments (Ericson, and others, 1956; figs. 2, 3) indicate that there was a well-defined change in climate from warmer than present to quite cold (glacial), some 60,000 to 50,000 years B.P.

Studies by Emiliani (1956, p. 281) indicated "that several temperature oscillations occurred during the Pleistocene epoch in superficial ocean waters of equatorial and tropical regions. The amplitude was found to be about 6° C. and the period about 41,000 years." The *end* of the last 41,000-year period was close to 11,000 years B.P. (cf. Broecker, 1957; p. 1703), and so, the beginning was some 52,000 years B.P.; that is, the beginning of a climatic change, from slightly warmer than present to glacial in nature, occurred about 52,000 years ago.[5] (It should be noted here that the locations of the ocean-bottom sediments which were studied by Ericson and others and by Emiliani could have been very nearly the same distance from the equator when the earth's North Pole stood in the position described in reading 364-1, A-1, as they are now. Also it is probable that none of the locations of the deep-sea cores [which were studied by the authors cited directly above] were within an area that would have comprised the now-submerged "Atlantean" continent.)

Sanderson (*Reader's Digest*, April, 1960) has studied the great fossil herds of woolly mammoths, woolly rhinoceroses, giant oxen, huge tigers, giant bisons, and so forth, found in parts of Alaska and Siberia. He concludes (1960, p. 124) that the animals were deep-frozen almost instantaneously in response to a very rapid slippage of the earth's crust that brought parts of the crust that had previously been at middle-latitude locations to much higher latitudes. In other words, he believes that "ice. . .[and]. . .the changing of the poles destroyed the animals."

Unfortunately, Sanderson postulates both crustal slippage and a climatic catastrophe to explain the extinction of the animals and suggests that both took place suddenly, about 10,000 years ago. In the case of the woolly mammoth, however, as well as many of the other giant animals, it is becoming clear that extinction occurred gradually throughout the last ice age.

Thus, a more acceptable hypothesis would involve the sequence: polar shift—resultant ice age—resultant gradual extinction of animals. And in terms of reincarnation theory it would still be possible for an "entity" to find, over the span of

5. Note: ". . .any attempt at time-extrapolation into the Pleistocene using deep-sea cores must be approached with a great deal of caution." (Broecker, et. al., 1958)

several lifetimes or incarnations, that this was indeed a sequence whose ultimate cause lay in the mechanism of polar shift.

10,500,000 B.P. to 17,600 B.P.

Q-3. How large was Atlantis during the time of Amilius [Adam]?
A-3. Comparison, that of Europe including Asia in Europe—not Asia, but Asia in Europe—see? This composed, as seen in or after the first of the destructions, that which would be termed now—with the present position—the southernmost portion of same—islands as created by those of the first (as man would call) volcanic or eruptive forces brought into play in the destruction of same.

Q-4. Was Atlantis one large continent, or a group of large islands?
A-4. Would it not be well to read that just given? Why confuse in the questionings? As has been given, what would be considered one large continent, until the first eruptions brought those changes—from what would now, with the present position of the earth in its rotation, or movements about its sun, through space, about Arcturus, about the Pleiades, [be] that of a whole or one continent. Then with the breaking up, producing more of the nature of large islands, with the intervening canals or ravines, gulfs, bays or streams... **364-6, February 17, 1932**

30,000 B.P. (28,000 B.C.)

... the entity ["entity" refers to the individual for whom the reading was given] was in Atlantis when there was the second period of disturbance—which would be some twenty-two thousand, five hundred (22,500) [years] before the periods of the Egyptian activity covered by the Exodus; or it was some twenty-eight thousand (28,000) [years] before Christ, see?
470-22, July 5, 1938

It would seem probable that "the second period of disturbance" referred to in the foregoing reading refers to the moral and spiritual "disturbances" outlined in reading 364-4 below, rather than to disturbances of a geological nature. A "first" period of disturbance would probably have been the invasion of Atlantis "by those of the animal kingdoms." (See 364-4 below.)

60,000 B.P. (?) to 17,000 B.P. (approximately)

Then, with the coming in or the raising up of Esai [?], with the change that had come about, began that period when there were the invasions of this continent [Atlantean] by those of the animal kingdoms, that brought about that meeting of the nations of the globe to prepare a way and manner of disposing of [these], else they be disposed of themselves by these forces. With this coming in, there came then the first of the destructive forces as could be set and then be meted out in its force or power. Hence, that as is termed, or its first beginning of, *explosives* that might be carried about, came with this reign, or this period, when *man*—or *men*, then—began to cope with those of the beast form that *overran* the earth in many places. Then, with these destructive forces, we find the first turning of the altar fires into that of sacrifice of those that were taken in the various ways, and human sacrifice began. With this also came the first egress of peoples to that of the Pyrenees first, *of* which later we find that peoples who enter into the black, or the mixed peoples, in what later became the Egyptian dynasty. We also find that entering into the Og, or those peoples that later became the beginning of the Inca, or Ohum, that builded the walls across the mountains in this period, through those same usages of that as had been taken on by those peoples; and with the same, those that made for that in the other land, became first those of the mound dwellers, or peoples in that land. With the continued disregard of those that were keeping the pure race and the pure peoples, of those that were to bring all these laws as applicable to the Sons of God, man brought in the destructive forces as used for the peoples that were to be the rule, that combined with those natural resources of the gases, of the electrical forces, made in nature and natural form the first of the eruptions that awoke from the depth of the slow cooling earth, and that portion now near what would be termed the Sargasso Sea first went into the depths . . .

364-4, February 16, 1932

The use of these influences by the Sons of Belial brought, then, the first of the upheavals; or the turning of the etheric rays' influence *from* the Sun—as used by the Sons of the Law of One—into the facet for the activities of same—produced what we would call a volcanic upheaval; and the separating of the land into *several* islands—five in number.

877-26, May 23, 1938

Q-2. What was the date of this first destruction, estimating in our present day system of counting time, in years B.C.?

A-2. Seven thousand five hundred (7,500) years before the final destruction, which came as has been given [approximately 8,150 B.C.]. 364-11, April 29, 1932

The above readings indicate that at about 17,600 B.P. a man-made eruption caused the portion of the Atlantean continent "near what would be termed the Sargasso Sea" to break up and founder. The Sargasso Sea is a "tract of the North Atlantic Ocean covered with floating seaweed...This tract is bounded approximately by 25° and 31°N by 40° and 70°W, but its extent and density are influenced by winds and ocean currents." (*Encyclopaedia Britannica,* 1956; v. 19, p. 998)

The idea that 17,600 years ago a civilization existed which was so technically advanced that it was capable of utilizing the *etheric rays* of the sun as a primary source of power is foreign to present-day concepts of human history. Recently, however, a bit of apparently factual evidence has been revealed which might support such a view. The evidence consists of very ancient maps of Greenland, Antarctica, and other portions of the world, maps which are highly accurate—so accurate in fact that in some instances they show mountain ranges which have since been found by the Army Map Service. What is the more remarkable is that they show both Greenland and Antarctica in an unglaciated state. This implies that the maps are many thousands of years old. Expeditions to Greenland and Antarctica have since verified (by means of seismic surveys) the subglacial topography depicted on these maps. The authority who solved the map projections, A.H. Mallery, thinks it possible that the ancient cartographers, who were superior in their abilities, might have accomplished their feats by mapping from the air.[6]

According to the readings, at any rate, the first of the destructions of Atlantis occurred about 17,000 years ago. The upheavals at this time were a result of the *second* introduction of "destructive forces." The first of the destructive forces coincides with the introduction of explosives cited above.

A life reading given for a brilliant, sensitive young scientist explains the mechanism of this first destruction of Atlantis.

6. Copies of the maps, together with a transcript of a radio broadcast which describes the pertinent facts of their discovery and the solving of their projections—as well as commentary by the seismologist, Rev. Daniel Linehan—are available from the Georgetown University Forum, Washington, D.C. The broadcast was made on August 26, 1956, and is entitled "New and Old Discoveries in Antarctica."

Q-1. Give an account of the electrical and mechanical knowledge of the entity, as Asal-Sine, in Atlantis.

A-1. Yes, we have the entity's activities during that experience. As indicated, the entity was associated with those that dealt with the mechanical appliances and their application during the experience. And, as we find, it was a period when there was much that has not even been thought of as yet in the present experiences.

About the firestone that was in the experience did the activities of the entity then make those applications that dealt with both the constructive and destructive forces in the period.

It would be well that there be given something of a description of this, that it may be better understood by the entity in the present, as to how both constructive and destructive forces were generated by the activity of this stone.

In the center of a building, that today would be said to have been lined with non-conductive metals, or non-conductive stone—something akin to asbestos, with the combined forces of bakerite [bakelite?] or other non-conductors that are now being manufactured in England under a name that is known well to many of those that deal in such things.

The building above the stone was oval, or a dome wherein there could be or was the rolling back, so that the activity of the stone was received from the sun's rays, or from the stars; the concentrating of the energies that emanate from bodies that are on fire themselves—with the elements that are found and that are not found in the earth's atmosphere. The concentration through the prisms or glass, as would be called in the present, was in such a manner that it acted upon the instruments that were connected with the various modes of travel, through induction methods—that made much the character of control as the remote control through radio vibrations or directions would be in the present day; though the manner of the force that was impelled from the stone acted upon the motivating forces in the crafts themselves.

There was the preparation so that when the dome was rolled back there might be little or no hindrance in the application direct to the various crafts that were to be impelled through space, whether in the radius of the visioning of the one eye, as it might be called, or whether directed under water or under other elements through other elements.

The preparation of this stone was in the hands only of the initiates at the time, and the entity was among those that directed the influences of the radiation that arose in the form of the rays that were invisible to the eye but that acted upon the stones themselves as set in the motivating forces—

whether the aircraft that were lifted by the gases in the period or whether guiding the more pleasure vehicles that might pass along close to the earth, or what would be termed the crafts on the water or under the water.

These, then, were impelled by the concentrating of the rays from the stone that was centered in the middle of the power station, or power house (that would be termed in the present).

In the active forces of these the entity brought destructive forces, by the setting up—in various portions of the land—the character that was to act as producing the powers in the various forms of the people's activities in the cities, the towns, the countries surrounding same. These, not intentionally, were *tuned* too high—and brought the second period of destructive forces to the peoples in the land, and broke up the land into the isles that later became the periods the further destructive forces were brought in the land.

Through the same form of fire the bodies of individuals were regenerated, by the burning—through the application of the rays from the stone, the influences that brought destructive forces to an animal organism. Hence the body rejuvenated itself often, and remained in that land until the eventual destruction, joining with the peoples that made for the breaking up of the land—or joining with Baalilal at the final destruction of the land. In this the entity lost. At first, it was not the intention nor desire for destructive forces. Later it was for the ascension of power itself.

As to describing the manner of construction of the stone, we find it was a large cylindrical glass (as would be termed today), cut with facets in such a manner that the capstone on top of same made for the centralizing of the power or force that concentrated between the end of the cylinder and the capstone itself.

As indicated, the records of the manners of construction of same are in three places in the earth, as it stands today: In the sunken portions of Atlantis, or Poseidia, where a portion of the temples may yet be discovered, under the slime of ages of sea water—near what is known as Bimini, off the coast of Florida. And in the temple records that were in Egypt, where the entity later acted in cooperation with others in preserving the records that came from the land where these had been kept. Also the records that were carried to what is now Yucatan in America, where these stones (that they know so little about) are now—during the last few months—*being* uncovered.

Ready for questions. . .

Q-2. *Is it for this entity to again learn the use of these stones?*

A-2. When there have come those individuals who will purify

75

themselves in the manner necessary for the gaining of the knowledge and the entering into the chambers where these may be found; yes—if the body will purify itself. In '38 it should come about, should the entity—or others may be raised.

In Yucatan there is the emblem of same. Let's clarify this, for it may be the more easily found—for they will be brought to this America, these United States. A portion is to be carried, as we find, to the Pennsylvania State Museum. A portion is to be carried to the Washington preservations of such findings, or to Chicago.

The stones that are set in the front of the temple, between the service temple and the outer court temple—or the priest activity, for later there arose (which may give a better idea of what is meant) the activities of the Hebrews from this—in the altar that stood before the door of the tabernacle. This altar or stone, then, in Yucatan, stands between the activities of the priest (for, of course, this is degenerated from the original use and purpose, but is the nearest and closest one to being found).

As to the use of same, and as to how it's to be applied, one must prepare self—and it may not wholly be given through any channel, until an individual has so purified his purposes and desires. For, as given [Genesis 9:11] not again will man bring to himself, or to those that have not been awakened to their individual development, destruction for the earth—saving man does it himself!

Q-3. What should be the nature of this purification?

A-3. Purifying from within, much in the way and manner as has been given or illustrated to the entity in how that the mental self must be purified, much in the same way and manner as the *inner* self has been purified through its sojourns in the planetary influences between the appearances in the earth. For, as given, the body, the body-consciousness, is a well-balanced body, mind and soul, *for* development as an initiate, to again use these forces, these influences, for *constructive* rather than destructive purposes.

440-5, December 20, 1933

12,658 B.P. (10,700 B.C.) [approximately]

In the latter portion of same we find as *cities* were builded more and more rare became those abilities to call upon the forces in nature to supply the needs for those of bodily adornment, or those of the needs to supply the replenishing of the wasting away of the physical being; or hunger arose, and with the determinations to set again in motion, we find there—then Ani [?], in those latter periods, ten thousand seven hundred (10,700) years before the Prince of Peace came—again was the bringing into forces that to *tempt* as it were, nature—in its storehouse—of replenishing the things—that of the *wasting* away in the mountains, then into the valleys, then into the sea itself; and the fast disintegration of the lands, as well as of the peoples—save those that had escaped into those distant lands.   364-4, February 16, 1932

Q-5. What were the principal islands called at the time of the final destruction?
A-5. Poseidia and Aryan [?], and Og [?].
                    364-6, February 17, 1932

12,500 B.P. (10,600 B.C.) [Reference to Yucatan]

From time as counted in the present we would turn back to 10,600 years before the Prince of Peace came into the land of promise . . .
But, understand, the surface was quite different from that which would be viewed in the present. For, rather than being a tropical area it was more of the temperate, and quite varied in the conditions and positions of the face of the areas themselves.   5750-1, November 12, 1933

The major climatic change that led from the cold glacial climate to the present earth climate occurred close to 11,000 years B.P. (Broecker, 1957, p. 1703) An estimate of the nature of the climate in Yucatan about 12,500 B.P. may be gained by comparison with the moist-indicator graphs shown in Sears and others. (1955) Values of moist maxima (periods of greater climatic moisture) were determined in a study of pollen from a long bog core taken near Mexico City (1 to 3 degrees of latitude south of Yucatan) and were correlated with temperature gradients (*ibid.*, fig. 4) in the general region. The work just cited indicates that at about 12,500 B.P. (within approximately the 16 to 20 m. depth in the core profile) the climate in the Mexico City region was cooler (cf. also, 1955, p. 1 and p. 523) and drier than at present. It would be expected that a similar condition would have obtained in Yucatan (some 700 miles almost due east) during this time; that is, the area of Yucatan would have been "more of the temperate" in climate.
The variation "in the conditions and positions of the face of the areas" is explained further along in the above reading where one reads that in "the final upheaval of Atlantis, or the islands that were later upheaved . . . much of the contour of the

77

land in Central America and Mexico was changed to that similar in outline to that which may be seen in the present." (5750-1) The "islands that were later upheaved" could be a reference to the Bahamas, as indicated by reading 364-3. Gravity anomalies in the Bahamas follow topographical trends and features. Worzel, and others (1953), believe that "the anomalies can be explained by ... construction of the shallow-water portions with regional compensation." The "construction of the shallow-water portions" (Bahamian platforms) could be due either to deposition or to *upheaval* of blocks of the crust.

12,448 to 12,348 B.P. (10,490 to 10,390 B.C.)

Q-5. What was the date of the actual beginning and ending of the construction of the Great Pyramid?
A-5. Was one hundred years in construction. Begun and completed in the period of Araaraart's time, with Hermes and Ra.
Q-6. What was the date B.C. of that period?
A-6. 10,490 to 10,390 before the Prince entered into Egypt.
                                        5748-6, July 1, 1932

Date of building of great pyramid of Gizeh: 4,700 B.C. (*Encyclopaedia Britannica,* 1956, v. 18, p. 793)

12,258 B.P. (10,300 B.C.) [approximately]

... the entity may be said to have been the first to begin the establishment of the library of knowledge in Alexandria; ten thousand three hundred [years] before the Prince of Peace ...
                                        315-4, June 18, 1934

11,950 B.P. (10,000 B.C.) [approximately]

...in that fair country of Alta, or Poseidia proper ... we find the entity in that sex as given, as was in the household of the ruler of that country ... This we find nearly ten thousand years before the Prince of Peace came ...
                                        288-1, November 20, 1923

7,450 B.P. (5,500 B.C.) [approximately]

...the entity was in Atlantis when there was the second period of disturbance—which would be some twenty-two thousand, five hundred (22,500) [years] before the periods of
78

the Egyptian activity covered by the Exodus; or it was some twenty-eight thousand (28,000) [years] before Christ, see? [Period covered by Exodus is 7458 B.P.]

470-22, July 5, 1938

"On the whole the most probable suggestion would throw the Exodus back to a point in or near the reign of Thothmes III and make the 15th century B.C. [3,548 B.P.] the earliest possible period." (*Encyclopaedia Britannica*, 1956, v. 8, p. 972)

4,060 to 3,560 B.P. (2,100 to 1,600 B.C.) [approximately]

...in the Holy Land when there were those breakings up in the periods when the land was being sacked by the Chaldeans and Persians ... among those groups who escaped in ships that settled in portions of the English land near what is now Salisbury, and there builded those altars that were to represent the dedications of individuals to the service of a living God. [Stonehenge?]   3645-1, January 15, 1944

"*Stonehenge,* a circular setting of large standing stones surrounded by an earthwork, situated about 8 mi. N. of Salisbury, Wiltshire, England . . . belonging to the late Neolithic period. This date is confirmed . . . by a radioactive carbon determination . . .(1848 B.C. plus or minus 275 years). [The structures] are unknown elsewhere in prehistoric northern Europe, and imply influence from the contemporary Mycenaean and Minoan architecture of the Mediterranean. The probability of such influence was startlingly confirmed in 1953. . ." (*Encyclopaedia Britannica*, 1956, v. 21, pp. 440-441)

"In the course of the 20th century B.C., the towns still left in Transjordan after generations of nomadic incursions seem to have been destroyed . . . This phase of devastation coincides closely with the first successful wave of north-west-Semitic [includes Chaldean] conquest . . . The incursions of desert nomads into western Palestine also led to destruction...west of the Jordan. By 1900 B.C., the population of Palestine had probably reached one of the lowest levels in its history. . ." (*Encyclopaedia Britannica*, 1956, v. 17, p. 125)

1926 A.D.

As for the weather conditions, and the effect same will produce on various portions of the earth's sphere, and this in its relation to the conditions in man's affairs: As has been oft

79

given, Jupiter and Uranus influences in the affairs of the world appear the strongest on or about October 15th to 20th when there may be expected in the minds, the actions—not only of individuals, but in various quarters of the globe—destructive conditions as well as building. In the affairs of man many conditions will arise that will be very, very strange to the world at present—in religion, in politics, in the moral conditions, and in the attempt to curb or to change such, see?...Violent wind storms—two earthquakes, one occurring in California, another in Japan—tidal waves following, one to the southern portion of the isles near Japan.

195-32, August 27, 1926

The following excerpts are from the *Monthly Weather Review* for October, 1926 (U.S. Weather Bureau, 1926): "October was an exceptionally stormy month and the number of days with gales was considerably above the normal over the greater part of the [North Atlantic] ocean. Several tropical disturbances occurred during the month, three of which were of slight intensity, but the storm that created such havoc in Cuba on the 20th was one of the most severe on record." (p. 435) In the vicinity of the Kuril Islands, "the westerly winds increased to hurricane force on the 14th and 15th..." Reports from ships in the vicinity of the Philippine Islands "indicate 3 and probably 4 violent storms [typhoons] during the early part of October, 1926." (p. 438) Reports of storms in the southern hemisphere for 1926 are difficult to obtain or lacking entirely. The closest one may come in most cases are the reports of the *India Weather Review*. This publication states (p. 110) that "a moderate storm occurred the 15th to the 18th of October in Andaman Sea."

The California earthquake of October 22, 1926, was composed of three strong shocks (up to magnitude VIII on Rossi-Forel scale; refer to this scale on p. 111) and "the principal shocks were perceptible over probably 100,000 square miles." (U.S. Coast and Geodetic Survey, 1951, p. 26) The previous strong shock reported (*ibid.*, p. 26) for California was on July 25, 1926, and the following strong shock was on January 1, 1927. Three earthquakes occurred in Japan on the 19th and 20th of October (Anon., 1926, pp. 340-342), but these were not relatively strong shocks and there were no pronounced *tidal waves following,* at least in the sense of tsunami, or seismic sea waves.

Another reading that bears upon California earthquakes and earthquakes in general follows:

Q-20. What is the primary cause of earthquakes? Will San Francisco suffer from such a catastrophe this year? If so, give date, time and information for the guidance of this body, who has personal property, records and a wife, all of which it wishes safety.

A-20. We do not find that this particular district (San Francisco) in the present year will suffer the great *material* damages that *have* been experienced heretofore. While portions of the country will be affected, we find these will be farther *east* than San Francisco—or those *south,* where there has *not* been heretofore the greater activity.

The causes of these, of course, are the movements about the earth; that is, internally—and the cosmic activity or influence of other planetary forces and stars and their relationships produce or bring about the activities of the elementals of the earth; that is, the Earth, the Air, the Fire, the Water—and those combinations make for the replacements in the various activities.   270-35, January 21, 1936

No strong shock was felt in all of California in 1936, the year of the above reading. (U.S. Coast and Geodetic Survey, 1951, p. 30) Published records (*ibid.,* pp. 30-35) indicate that all of the eight principal shocks in California and Nevada, for the period 1936 to 1950, were to the southeast of San Francisco.

The concept of "cosmic influence" as an element to be considered in the mechanism of earthquakes has recently been proposed by Tomaschek. (1960) He writes (p. 338): "To state the plain facts: one is led to the conclusion that the position of Uranus within 15° of the meridian at the moment of great earthquakes can be regarded as significant and that there exist times of longer period (several years) when it is very highly significant. It is quite obvious that the strains and stresses in the earth's crust are the primary cause of earthquakes, but it has been shown. . .that the *timing* of the event can be described by the position of Uranus. If it is necessary to explain this within the limits of present-day science, attention should be directed to the fact that Uranus is the only planet of which the direction of its axis of rotation coincides with the plane of its orbital revolution. A possible magnetic field would influence the solar plasma in a way quite different from all the other planets.

"The earthquake which destroyed Agadir. . .occurred with Uranus only about 4° from the meridian. Anybody in Agadir, knowing of my communication in *Nature*. . .would have kept away from buildings at the time of Uranus being near the meridian of Agadir which was from about 10 hrs. to 12 hrs. a.m. or p.m. The destruction of the town occurred at 11 hrs. p.m. local time. An unbiased approach to these problems, of which the correlations of Uranus are only a part and a first step, may help humanity."

There was an interesting sidelight to the weather predictions made by Mr. Cayce around 1926. In one reading the question was asked:

Q-1. Is Herbert Janvrin Browne's theory correct—whereby weather is forecasted several years in advance by measuring solar radiation and its action on the ocean currents?

A-1. Were these various accounts considered of that information intimated here, these would be *not* correct, for *this* may be established as a *theory:* That thrown off will be returned. As the heat or cold in the various parts of the earth is radiated off, and correlated with reflection in the earth's atmosphere, and *this* in *its* action changes the currents or streams in the ocean; and the waters bring or carry the heat in a manner to the various shores, or bring cold or carry cold to the various shores.   195-29, May 28, 1926

It is perhaps noteworthy, therefore, that one of the leading theories of climatic change, the carbon-dioxide theory, reads as follows: "The carbon dioxide theory states that, as the amount of carbon-dioxide increases, the atmosphere becomes opaque over a larger frequency interval; the outgoing radiation is trapped more effectively near the earth's surface and the temperature rises. The latest calculations show that if the carbon dioxide content of the atmosphere should double, the surface temperature would rise 3.6°C. . . " (Plass, 1956, p. 303)

1932-1962 A.D.

With the years that are to come, conditions that are to arise, as we find, eventually—and this within the next thirty years— Norfolk, with its environs, is to be the chief port on the East coast, this not excepting Philadelphia or New York; the second being rather in the New England area.

5541-2, July 27, 1932

In 1957 Norfolk harbor and the port of Newport News together shipped and imported a total of 59,920 thousand short tons of cargo. Ports of the "Delaware River and tributaries" were second with 47,569; New York harbor was third with 42,003; Baltimore harbor and channels, Md., handled 32,044; and Portland harbor, Me., was fifth with 12,935. (U.S. Bureau Census, 1959, table 776)

1935 A.D. and beyond

Q-12. Regarding general world conditions, is it likely that changes in the earth's surface in the Mediterranean area, will stop Italy's campaign against Ethiopia?
A-12. Not at *this* particular period. This may *eventually* be a portion of the experience, but not just yet.
Q-13. When is this likely to occur?
A-13. As to times and places and seasons, as it has indeed been indicated in the greater relationships that have been established by the prophets and sages of old—and especially as given by Him: "As to the day and hour, who knoweth? *No one,* save the Creative Forces."
Tendencies in the hearts and souls of men are such that these [upheavals] may be brought about. For, as often indicated through these channels oft, it is not the world, the earth, the environs about it nor the planetary influences, not the associations or activities, that *rule* man. *Rather* does man—by *his* compliance with divine law—bring *order* out of chaos; or, by his *disregard* of the associations and laws of divine influence, bring chaos and *destructive* forces into his experience.
For *He* hath given, "Though the heavens and the earth pass away, my *word* shall *not* pass away!" This is oft considered just a beautiful saying, or something to awe those who have been stirred by some experience. But applying them into the conditions that exist in the affairs of the world and the universe in the present, what *holds* them—what are the foundations of the earth? The word of the Lord!

416-7, October 7, 1935

Q-2. Please forecast the principal events for the next fifty years affecting the welfare of the human race.
A-2. This had best be cast after the great catastrophe that's coming to the world in '36 (thirty-six), in the form of the breaking up of many *powers* that now exist as factors in the world affairs. . .Then, with the breaking up in '36 (thirty-six) will be the *changes* that will make different *maps* of the world.
Q-8. Will Italy adopt a more liberal form of government in the near future?
A-8. Rather that of a more monarchal government than that

of the liberal. Italy, too, will be broken by what *now* is an insignificant or small power that lies *between* those of the other *larger* or those of the *moment* that are of the larger. These will not come as we find, as broken, before the catastrophes of outside forces to the earth in '36, which will come from the shifting of the equilibrium of the earth itself in space, with those of the consequential effects upon the various portions of the country—or world—affected by same.

3976-10, February 8, 1932

Q-10. What will be the type and extent of the upheaval in '36?
A-10. The wars, the upheavals in the interior of the earth, and the shifting of same by the differentiation in the axis as respecting the positions from the Polaris center.

5748-6, July 1, 1932

The above two readings are of the utmost importance to the understanding of subsequent readings that predict great changes in the earth's geography and near cataclysmic geologic events. They point to an immediate (terrestrial) mechanism underlying the proposed earth changes—namely, a shift of the earth's axis of rotation, or a shifting of the interior of the earth with respect to the rotational axis.

Gold (1955) has considered the consequences of instability of the earth's axis of rotation and concluded that the effects of shift of the rotational axis can be of considerable consequence in the rapid deformation of the crust of the earth. The geophysicist, Vening Meinesz, concludes that previous polar shifts "could not have taken place without currents in the mantle" of the earth's interior. (Heiskanen and Vening Meinesz, p. 453)

Markowitz (Runcorn, 1960, p. 348) presents a table showing the observed mean latitudes of the five International Latitude Service stations for the mean epochs 1903, 1909, 1915, 1927, 1932, 1938, and 1952. Accounting for unequal time differences between epochs, it shows that the greatest differences in observed positions for all five stations occurred between mean epochs 1932 and 1938. Perhaps such differences in some way reflect *shifting of the equilibrium of the earth itself in space,* in 1936.

In a paper discussing the remarkable occurrence of rises and ridges along the midlines of ocean basins throughout the world, Menard (1958, pp. 1183-1184) states: "The process that centers rises in ocean basins has the following characteristics:

84

(1) It is sensitive to the margins of the basins;

(2) It is capable of acting at distances as great as half the width of the Pacific basin. . .

(3) It acts on both sides of a basin at one time;

(4) It appears to be ephemeral or intermittent.

"One possible process is the convection current. If so, the high heat-flow along seismically active rises implies *rising currents* [author's italics] in the middle. . .Continuity requires sinking currents near the margins of the basins. . ."

Indeed, in a report of recent deep-sea expeditions in the Pacific, "it was found that in regions of uplift of the earth's crust beneath the oceans, such as Easter Island Rise. . .the heat flow was larger than normal. Near regions of severe down-warping of the crust, in the vicinity of the South American Trench along the western edge of the continent, for example, the values were much lower than expected. These findings support the theory that great convection currents exist within the earth's mantle." These currents "may actually be the cause of the uplifts and downwarps." (Trans. Amer. Geophys. Union, v. 39, 1958, p. 1013)

It would seem that "upheavals in the interior of the earth" (convection currents?) could, in a few years, bring about many of the *rising* and *sinking* land movements described in some of the readings that follow.

1936 A.D. and beyond

Q-29. Are there to be physical changes in the earth's surface in Alabama?

A-29. Not for some period yet.

Q-30. When will the changes begin?

A-30. Thirty-six to thirty-eight.

Q-31. What part of the State will be affected?

A-31. The northwestern part, and the extreme south-western part.   311-9, August 6, 1932

Q-14. Are the physical changes in Alabama predicted for 1936-38 to be gradual or sudden changes?

A-14. Gradual.

Q-15. What form will they take?

A-15. To be sure, that may depend upon much that deals with metaphysical, as well as to that people call actual or in truth! for as understood—or should be [understood] by the entity—there are those conditions that in the activity of individuals, in line of thought and endeavor, keep oft many a city and many a land intact through their application of the spiritual laws in their associations with individuals. This will take more of the form here in the change, as we find, through the sinking of portions, with the following up of the inundations by this overflow.   311-10, November 19, 1932

1958 A.D.—Norfolk-Virginia Beach, Virginia, area

Q-16. What, if any, changes will take place around Norfolk area, Va.?
A-16. No *material*, that would be effective to the area, other than would eventually become more beneficial—in a port, and the like.   311-8, April 9, 1932

Q-16. When will the physical changes start in Norfolk and vicinity?
A-16. This would be nearer to '58 than to '38 or '36, as we find.   311-10, November 19, 1932

The opening of the Hampton Roads Bridge Tunnel took place in 1957, and in October of this same year approval was granted for construction of the 200-million-dollar Chesapeake Bay Bridge Tunnel. As the longest fixed-crossing in the world, this structure would make the Norfolk area a sort of "port" for auto and truck traffic along the east coast. In 1959, the engineering and cost analyses for two huge new general cargo facilities at Newport News and Norfolk were completed.

Q-3. What is the future of Virginia Beach?
A-3. ....as we would give, of all the resorts that are in the East coast, Virginia Beach will be the first and the longest lasting of the increasing of the population, valuation, and activities. Hence, as we would give, the future is *good*.
                                5541-2, July 27, 1932

Q-19. Virginia Beach is to be safe, then?
A-19. It is the center—and the only seaport and center—of the White Brotherhood.   1152-11, August 12, 1941

1958 A.D.—Anti-gravity?

Q-14. How was this particular Great Pyramid of Gizeh built?
A-14. By the use of those forces in nature as make for iron to swim. Stone floats in the air in the same manner. This will be discovered in '58.   5748-6, July 1, 1932

86

Professor W. Heisenberg announces (1958) discovery of a unified-field theory which relates mass, energy and gravity. Professor L.I. Schiff (*Chicago Daily News,* May 1, 1958, p. 11) states: "...gravitation may be explicable in some other way than by Einstein's general theory of relativity," and suggests that gravitational force may come from the constant swapping of minute, weightless neutrinos. Schiff (1958) also reports on the gravitational properties of anti-matter. (*Science,* p. 1149)

Weber (1959) reports on work done in 1958 on the detection and generation of gravitational waves, stating (p. 306): "...methods are proposed [for the generation of gravitational waves], which employ electrically induced stresses in crystals. These give approximately a seventeen-order increase in radiation over a spinning rod of the same length as the crystals." Furth (1960, p. 387) reports on recent experiments with magnetic pressure, which "can move mountains of metal or plasma for the engineer, and atoms for the physicist." Finally, Dirac (1959, p. 924) presents an analysis he worked out in 1958 that leads to a better understanding of Einstein's equations for the gravitational field.

The foregoing are among several of the promising possibilities that might be listed as evidence that the basic understanding of forces that could make stone float *in the air* may have been discovered in 1958.

1958-1998 A.D.

As to the changes physical again: The earth will be broken up in the western portion of America. The greater portion of Japan must go into the sea. The upper portion of Europe will be changed as in the twinkling of an eye. Land will appear off the east coast of America. There will be the upheavals in the Arctic and in the Antarctic that will make for the eruption of volcanoes in the Torrid areas, and there will be the shifting then of the poles—so that where there have been those of a frigid or semi-tropical will become the more tropical, and moss and fern will grow. And these will begin in those periods in '58 to '98, when these will be proclaimed as the periods when His Light will be seen again in the clouds.

3976-15, January 19, 1934

Miyabe (1953) reports measurements that indicate that vertical displacement has taken place along the tectonic median line of southwest Japan. Iida and Wada (1955)

87

calculate that subsidence in the Ise bay region, Honshu, on the east coast of south-central Japan, is progressing at the rate of from two to six centimeters annually. Ishii (1955) concluded that subsidence along the coast of Toyama Bay, which caused the submergence of a forest, was due to movement of a block of the crust. (All of the foregoing might well be expected in such a geologically instable region as Japan.)

"In the countries bordering the Baltic Sea an uplift has been under observation for a long period. . .raised beaches and other shoreline features indicate that. . .parts of Sweden and Finland are at least 900 feet higher than they were at the close of the Ice Age." (Longwell, *et al.*, 1939, p. 315) The inference to be drawn here is that the overall geological trend, of uplift, in northern Europe may be the one being referred to by the psychic information. It is in the advocation of a very rapid acceleration of this trend that the psychic information departs from the standard geological concept of gradual change. It is also perhaps possible that if land appears "off the east coast of America," the upper portion of Europe could be changed "in the twinkling of an eye" by sudden blockage or diversion of the Gulf Stream that brings warmth to upper Europe.

Q-12. How soon will the changes in the earth's activity begin to be apparent?
A-12. When there is the first breaking up of some conditions in the South Sea (that's South Pacific, to be sure), and those as apparent in the sinking or rising of that that's almost opposite same, or in the Mediterranean, and the Aetna [Etna?] area, then we may know it has begun.

Q-13. How long before this will begin?
A-13. The indications are that some of these have already begun, yet others would say these are only temporary. We would say they have begun. . .

Q-14. Will there be any physical changes in the earth's surface in North America? If so, what sections will be affected, and how?
A-14. All over the country we will find many physical changes of a minor or greater degree. The greater change, as we will find, in America, will be the North Atlantic Seaboard. Watch New York! Connecticut, and the like.

Q-15. When will this be?
A-15. In this period. As to just when. . .

311-8, April 9, 1932

The Etna area, Sicily, is geologically active, as well known from the recent (July, 1960) and many historical eruptions of Mt. Etna and the great earthquake in the vicinity of the Strait of Messina, which occurred in 1908. In addition, strong, deep-focus earthquakes are known from the Mediterranean region.

The area of the South Pacific that is "almost opposite" the "Mediterranean, and the Aetna [Etna?] area" where "the first breaking up" will occur, would correspond to the area of great seismic activity that is centered at approximately 175°E long. and 20°S lat. (Richter, 1958, figs. 25-3, 25-4)

The perplexing statement about "the sinking or rising" in the Mediterranean area may possibly be connected with the recent water level drop in Greek harbors. The drop would indicate *rising* of the land in this eastern part of the Mediterranean. The following Reuters dispatch from Athens may be of significance:

"The water level in Greek harbors has been dropping recently, but scientists have been unable to explain why. The drop, which in many places exceeded three feet, first was noted after strong northerly winds and a drop in temperature. At Nafplion Harbor, in Southern Greece, small boats 'sat' on the sea bottom after the level of the waters fell by three feet. This low level was constant for a week. At Tolos, near Nafplion, fishing boats have had difficulty in approaching the wharves. The bottom of the old Venetian harbor at Heraklion, Crete, has appeared in many places. This has hampered pumping of water for cooling of equipment at the local electricity plant, endangering the town's electric power supply. Similar phenomena were reported from Rhodes Island, in the Southeast and Lefkas Island, off the western coast of Greece. The Hydrographic Service has ordered regular reports on sea levels from all harbor masters. Some attributed the drop to strong winds or to an undersea earthquake. However, the water level remained low even after the winds subsided. While no earthquake was recorded by seismographs." (*St. Louis Globe-Democrat*, June 5, 1959)

The earth will be broken up in many places. The early portion will see a change in the physical aspect of the west coast of America. There will be open waters appear in the northern portions of Greenland. There will be new lands seen off the Caribbean Sea, and *dry* land will appear. . .South America shall be shaken from the uppermost portion to the

end, and in the Antarctic off Tierra Del Fuego, *land,* and a
strait with rushing waters.   3976-15, January 19, 1934

If land is to appear off Tierra Del Fuego, then its appearance
will undoubtedly be associated with earth tremors of some sort.
In this regard, the following newspaper article may be of
significance:

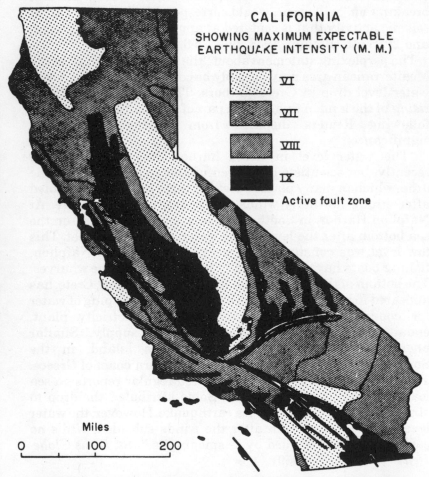

CALIFORNIA

SHOWING MAXIMUM EXPECTABLE
EARTHQUAKE INTENSITY (M. M.)

VI
VII
VIII
IX

Active fault zone

Miles

0   100   200

Figure 2—Seismic regionalization map for California, after Richter.
(1958, fig. 3) Notation "M.M." refers to the "modified Mercalli" scale
of earthquake intensity. On this scale an earthquake of VI is felt by all,
chimneys are damaged, but damage is generally slight. A quake of
intensity IX produces considerable damage, even in specially
designed structures, and the ground is cracked and underground pipes
are broken. A quake of XII rating is the greatest possible on this scale
and involves total damage. Refer to scale on p. 111.

"An earthquake, where there has never before been earthquakes, has been detected.

"A large 'quake took place recently in the northern Magellan Straits near the tip of South America.

"This is unusual, Jim Lander of the U.S. Coast and Geodetic Survey told Science Service, since there has never been an earthquake that far north in the Straits. Previously there had been a gap in a chain of earthquakes occurring in the region. The most recent one, tentatively located at 72 degrees west longitude and 51 degrees south latitude, fills in the gap which had extended from 47 to 53 degrees south latitude.

"Although only 12 northern stations reported the earthquake, there are good indications, Lander said, that it was a deep one and quite strong—estimated at well over six on the seismograph scale which runs from 0, just barely detectable, to 8.5." (*Norfolk Ledger-Dispatch,* July 16, 1959)

Q-2. I have for many months felt that I should move away from New York City.

A-2. This is well, as indicated. There is too much unrest; there will continue to be the character of vibrations that to the body will be disturbing, and eventually those destructive forces there—though these will be in the next generation.

Q-3. Will Los Angeles be safe?

A-3. Los Angeles, San Francisco, most all of these will be among those that will be destroyed before New York even.

Q-4. Should California or Virginia Beach be considered at all, or where is the right place that God has already provided for me to live?

A-4. As indicated, these choices should be made rather in self. Virginia Beach or the area is much safer as a definite place. But the work of the entity should embrace most all of the areas from the east to the west coast, in its persuading—not as a preacher, nor as one bringing a message of doom, but as a loving warning to all groups, clubs, women's clubs, writer's clubs, art groups, those of every form of club, that there needs be—in their activities—definite work towards the power of the Son of God's activity in the affairs of men.

1152-11, August 13, 1941

If there are the greater activities in the Vesuvius, or Pelée, then the southern coast of California—and the areas between Salt Lake and the southern portions of Nevada—may expect, within the three months following same, an inundation by the earthquakes.

The predicted destruction of Los Angeles and San Francisco mentioned above is, of course, impossible to treat objectively. For those who live in California, however, it might be of value to reproduce a map, compiled by the seismologist C.F. Richter, that gives a general picture of the earthquake intensities that may be expected (on the basis of past shocks) from place to place in the state. Prof. Richter's map (fig. 2) indicates, among other things, that active faults are present both in the San Francisco Bay area and in the Los Angeles basin. Activity along these faults, in response to movements beneath the earth's crust, could prove disastrous for these cities. An equally formidable menace could be the tsunami, or sea wave, that is generated by a submarine earthquake. Perhaps the "inundation" of the southern coast of California, mentioned in the above reading, refers to an inundation by tsunami. The tsunami that developed in response to the Chilean earthquakes of May, 1960, are well known, as is their destructive power; for example, "at the height of a tidal wave [a tsunami that was generated by the Chilean quake of May 21, 1960] that inundated the small port town of Corral. . .an 11,000 deadweight-ton cargo vessel 'actually floated over the town before being carried back to the sea again by the current'. . ." (*The New York Times,* July 10, 1960, p. 61)

From Prof. Richter's map (fig. 2) it can be seen that areas of seismic intensity sufficient to initiate tsunami exist off the coast of southern California. In another of Richter's maps (fig. 3) it can be seen that Salt Lake lies in a belt of relatively high seismicity, and so also does Lake Mead in southern Nevada. Presumably, earthquakes of great magnitude could result in displacement of the waters of these lakes, sufficient to inundate portions of "the areas between Salt Lake and the southern portions of Nevada." Or perhaps by "inundation," an overwhelming number of earthquakes is implied.

About the possible effects of future earthquakes on the buildings in downtown Los Angeles, the seismologist Richter has some interesting observations. He relates that, until lately, Los Angeles enforced a building-height limit of 13 stories, originally intended not as an earthquake safety measure but as a preventative of congestion in narrow streets. This general limit has recently been raised to 20 stories. Richter thinks this action was ill-advised, in view of the damage done to existing taller structures by the earthquake of 1952, and the record of larger motions of the same kind in 1857.

Dr. Richter points out that there is a general impression that earthquake risk does not exist at San Diego, historical records to the contrary being forgotten or ignored. And he suggests that the degree of potential shaking at San Francisco must be revised upward, because of the proximity of the great San Andreas fault, which passes just outside the city limits, only 8 miles from the business center.

1941-1998 A.D.

As to conditions in the geography of the world, of the country, changes here are gradually coming about.

...many portions of the east coast will be disturbed, as well as many portions of the west coast, as well as the central portion of the U.S.

In the next few years lands will appear in the Atlantic as well as in the Pacific. And what is the coast line now of many a land will be the bed of the ocean. Even many of the battlefields of the present [1941] will be ocean, will be the seas, the bays, the lands over which the *new* order will carry on their trade one with another.

Portions of the now east coast of New York, or New York City itself, will in the main disappear. This will be another generation, though, here; while the southern portions of Carolina, Georgia—these will disappear. This will be much sooner.

The waters of the lakes [Great Lakes] will empty into the Gulf [Gulf of Mexico], rather than the waterway over which such discussions have been recently made [St. Lawrence Seaway]. It would be well if the waterway were prepared, but not for that purpose for which it is at present being considered.

Then the area where the entity [1152] is now located [Virginia Beach] will be among the safety lands, as will be portions of what is now Ohio, Indiana and Illinois and much of the southern portion of Canada and the eastern portion of Canada; while the western land, much of that is to be disturbed—in this land—as, of course, much in other lands.

1152-11, August 13, 1941

Both horizontal and vertical changes in the earth's crust have taken place in geologically recent times, both on the east and west coasts. (Longwell, *et al.*, 1939, pp. 317, 318) "In 1811 large areas of the Mississippi flood plain near New Madrid, Missouri, sank far below their former level." (*Ibid.*, p. 317)

Two reading excerpts, for a man who owned a clothing business in New York City, have a bearing upon the foregoing readings (311-8 and 1152-11) that predict the *disappearance* of that community.

Q-8. Is the present location of business safe until the expiration of the lease [Jan. 1943]?

A-8. As indicated, after that period change to other environs—these on the mainland, not on Manhattan Island.

412-13, January 23, 1942

Q-13. Should the danger of bombing or any other upheaval be given any consideration in making this decision?

A-13. Not for the present.   412-15, September 24, 1942

Although the mechanism involved in the predicted destruction of the main part of New York City is not given in detail, it is perhaps of value to cite Richter's remarks (1959, p. 156) in regard to what is known of earthquake possibilities for this area. He indicates that New York City is within the range of VIII, on average ground, from a great earthquake in the St. Lawrence area. (Refer to fig. 3, this study.) A shock that occurred in 1884 confirms the presence of a local source of earthquakes capable of producing VIII and, locally, IX.

"...lands will appear in the Atlantic as well as in the Pacific": Presumably such uplift would be isostatically compensated by sinking of adjacent land areas (like the portions of the east coast, Carolina and Georgia, which are mentioned). Davis, and others (1959), state: Precise leveling by the Coast and Geodetic Survey in 1918, 1933, 1935, and 1955 indicates that the land surface has subsided as much as 4 inches in the Savannah, Georgia, area. Comparison of level lines of different periods indicates that most of the subsidence has taken place since 1933. Ground-water withdrawals are cited as the cause of subsidence, in this case.

After the Agadir earthquake of 1960, Tillotson wrote (1960, p. 199): "Evidence of a tremendous submarine upheaval off the coast was obtained from preliminary naval soundings. In one case the depth of water was found to be 45 ft. where previously it was chartered at 1,200 ft. In a position about 9 miles from shore, soundings showed a depth of 1,200 ft. instead of the charted 4,500 ft." An article in *The New York Times* (March 27, 1960) datelined Quito, Ecuador, stated: "An island more than a mile long, 100 yards wide and 125 feet high at some points has emerged from the Pacific off Ecuador. Two witnesses to the island's birth. . .said it was heralded by trembling of the earth and underground noises."

Finally, the following quote is pertinent with reference to the statement that "The waters of the lakes will empty into the Gulf." Once again, it is seen that a general geological trend is involved, but that the psychic information would accelerate the *rate* of geologic change. "An excellent example of tilting on a large scale is afforded by the Great Lakes. To the northeast the land has risen since the disappearance of the great ice sheet, and as a result the lake basins have been tilted southwestward." (*Ibid.*, p. 317) "The tilting movement is still in progress and has been accurately determined; it is at the rate of 5 inches per hundred miles per century. Small as this rate seems, in 1600 years it would cause the upper Great Lakes to discharge by way of the Chicago River into the Mississippi drainage." (*Ibid.*, p. 318)

In the later part of reading 1152-11 above, there is a reference to "safety lands," being composed of portions of Ohio, Indiana,

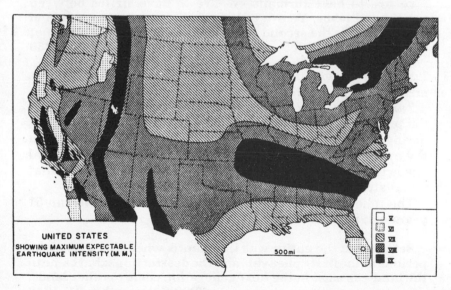

Figure 3—Tentative seismic regionalization map for the United States and adjacent areas, after Richter. (1958, fig. 4) Refer to scale on p. 111 for meaning of numerical designation of earthquake intensities.

and Illinois; much of the southern and eastern portions of Canada; and the Virginia Beach area. A glance at figure 3 shows that there is some support for such an interpretation, in terms of the historical pattern of earthquakes throughout the country—that is, all of the safety areas mentioned in the reading are in zones of relatively low seismic activity and intensity of the earthquakes is also relatively weak.

Strifes will arise through the period. Watch for them near the Davis Strait, in the attempts there for the keeping of the lifeline to a land open. Watch for them in Libya and in Egypt, in Ankara and in Syria, through the straits about those areas above Australia in the Indian Ocean and the Persian Gulf.

Ye say that these are of the sea; yes, for there shall the breaking up be, until there are those in every land that shall say that this or that shows the hand of divine interference, or that nature is taking a hand, or that it is the natural consequence of good judgments.

But in all of these [times], let each declare Whom ye will serve: a nation, a man, a state, or thy God?
                                        3976-26, April 28, 1941

Ye are to have turmoils—ye are to have strifes between capital and labor. Ye are to have a division in thy own land before there is the second of the Presidents that next will not live through his office—a mob rule!   3976-24, June 16, 1939

Strifes throughout the period—unfortunately most of these predictions have come true. No "breaking up" has taken place.

Turmoils. . .second of the Presidents. . .a mob rule! Here again the prediction of *strife* has come true. The existing president during this reading was Roosevelt. Whether the "division in thy own land" refers to a geological, sociological, or spiritual one is indeterminable, but it is believed by some students that racial strife was meant.

The following is found in a reading given for a woman 51 years old, in 1943:

Before that the entity was in Atlantis when there were the periods of the first upheavals and the destructions that came to the land—as must in the next generation come to other lands.
                                        3209-2, December 31, 1943

Another, given in 1944 for a 27-year-old woman, states:

. . .Changes are due to be wrought in the earth through the period of the entity's sojourn.   3648-1, January 24, 1944

An implication was given in a 1942 reading that there may be need for raising food to supplement that grown by farmers.

Q-11. Should I hold the 25 acres of land near Oceana, [Va.]; also, two sites in Linkhorn Park and lots on 54th St. [Va. Beach, Va.]?
A-11. Hold them until at least early spring; that is, the lots. Hold the acreage; for that may be the basis for the extreme periods through which all portions of the country must pass—for production for self as well as those closer associated with the body.   416-17, November 5, 1942

A further note on the production of food is found in this reading:

All that is for the sustenance of life *is* produced from the soil. Then there must be a return to the soil. Every man must be in that position that he at least creates, by his activities, that which will sustain the body—from the soil; or where he is supplying same to those activities that bring such experiences into the lives of all.   3976-19, June 24, 1938

1968-1969 A.D.

And Poseidia will be among the first portions of Atlantis to rise again. Expect it in sixty-eight and sixty-nine ('68 and '69); not so far away!   958-3, June 28, 1940

Yet, as time draws nigh when changes are to come about, there may be the opening of those three places where the records are one, to those that are the initiates in the knowledge of the One God: The temple [on Atlantis]. . .will *rise again.* Also there will be the opening of the temple or hall of records in Egypt, and those records that were put into the heart of the Atlantean land may also be found there. . .The *records* are *One.*   5750-1, November 12, 1933

Q-5. Could the well in Bimini be promoted and reconstructed?
A-5. There has been much given through this source [996] as to how that particular portion of what was the Atlantean period might be developed. While it would make for much

outlay in money, as ordinarily termed, there are certain interests that would join *in* such an undertaking. As those of the Dodge interests, as given. For it could be established as a center for two particular purposes; a regeneration for those with certain types of individual ailments (not only from the well, or water from same, but from the surrounding waters— because of the life in same), and a center for archaeological research. And as such activities are begun, there will be found much more gold in the lands under the sea than there is in the world circulation today!

As to how, this should be considered seriously from many varied angles that exist. For, as understood, there are those conditions as related to the varied powers that are in power or in affluence as respecting activities of any nature there. And as they exist in the present there are some complications for agreements, contracts, the lettings of this, that or the other.

But this should *not* be left alone; it should be considered from many angles.

Also aid may be induced from the varied societies that have been formed for the study of geological and archaeological activities, or such. For much will be found.

And, as may be known, when the changes begin, these portions will rise among the first.   587-4, July 1, 1935

According to Funk and Wagnalls *New College Standard Dictionary* (1947), Bimini refers to either of two small islands of the Bahama group, fabled to contain "the fountain of youth" sought by Ponce de Leon.

2000 to 2001 A.D.

Q-9. What great change or the beginning of what change, if any, is to take place in the earth in the year 2000 to 2001 A.D.?

A-9. When there is a shifting of the poles. Or a new cycle begins.   826-8, August 11, 1936

The "shifting of the poles" of the earth as a logical consequence of large-scale crustal displacements, like those predicted for the period 1958 to 2001, has been treated by Gold (1955, p. 528): "If a continent of the size of South America were suddenly raised by 30 meters, an angle of separation of the two axes of the order of one-hundreth of a degree would result. The plastic flow would then amount to a movement of one-thousandth of a degree per annum. The earth would hence topple over at a rate of one degree per thousand years or by a large angle in about 10^5 years. . .It is thus tempting to suggest that there have been just a few occasions when the axis has been 'free' and has swung around as rapidly as would be given by the stiffness of the earth and the rates of tectonic movement, leading to a timescale of the order of 10^5 or 10^6 years, but scarcely longer."

Comments and Conclusions

The psychic data quoted in this article were all on record prior to the passing of Mr. Cayce in 1945. At the time the psychic information was given, very little of it could have been rigorously compared with available scientific information. Recently, however, scientific inquiry has succeeded in treating a few of the subjects requisite for comparisons. Radiocarbon dating,[7] for instance, permits some of the quantitative time comparisons cited in the text. This method[8] of dating geologic materials, incidentally, has cut the length of time allotted (previous to about 1950) to the Pleistocene epoch by nearly 50 percent. Thus, prior to about 1950, any of the psychic dates cited above would have been considered too recent even to be worthy of comparisons. Deep-sea studies (including ionium dating) and paleomagnetic research are two more examples of scientific fields that have developed sufficiently since the 1920s and 1930s to permit meaningful comparisons.

On the basis of the comparisons given in this article, it would seem reasonable to say that some of the psychic data in the files of the Edgar Cayce Foundation, which previously could not be evaluated scientifically, now appear to compare well with "known facts." Favorable comparison alone, it is realized, does not necessarily render them true. Other psychic data do not agree with current scientific concepts. It would seem, however, that it is no longer necessary to accept some psychic statements on faith alone.

Most of the psychic statements quoted here are *at present* not amenable to scientific evaluation. This is in contrast to many "physical" readings which Mr. Cayce gave for people in ill health, that were accurate in detail (as evidenced and

---

7. Possibilities of the method first pointed out in 1946 by W.F. Libby.

8. Briggs, L.J., and Weaver, K.F., 1958. "How Old Is It?" *National Geographic,* v. 114, pp. 234-244; p. 240; figure explains how radiocarbon "works."

documented after examination by an M.D. or D.O.).

We are now entering a period when more extensive scientific evaluation of these readings will be possible. We are also entering a period in which the possibility exists that many of the psychic statements may be directly verified (as some have already been). It would seem advisable to enter the period with open minds, with the reservation that if these readings *are* verified in an experiential way, it is reasonable to assume that the remaining readings are equally valid.

REFERENCES

Anders, E., and Limber, D.N. "Origin of the Worzel Deep-sea Ash," *Nature,* v. 184, 1959, pp. 44-45.

Anonymous. "International Seismological Summary for 1926."

Anonymous. "Underwater Discoveries in the Straits of Florida," *Military Engineer,* v. 51, no. 343, 1959, p. 403.

Bramlette, M.N., and Bradley, W.H. "Geology and Biology of North Atlantic Deep-sea Cores Between Newfoundland and Ireland. Pt. 1: Lithology and Geologic Interpretations," *U.S. Geol. Survey,* Prof. Paper No. 196-A, 1940, pp. 1-34.

Broecker, W.S. "Evidence for a Major Climatic Change Close to 11,000 Years B.P." *Bull. Geol. Soc. America,* v. 68, 1957, pp. 1703-1704.

Broecker, W.S., and Kulp, J.L. "Lamont Natural Radio-carbon Measurements IV," *Science,* v. 126, 1957, pp. 1324-1334.

Broecker, W.S., and others. "The Relation of Deep-sea Sedimentation Rates to Variations in Climate," *Amer. Jour. Sci.,* v. 256, 1958, pp. 503-517.

_____ "Evidence for an Abrupt Change in Climate Close to 11,000 Years Ago," *Amer. Jour. Sci.,* v. 258, 1960, pp. 429-448.

Brooks, C.E.P. *Climate Through the Ages.* London: Ernest Bend, 1949, 395 pp.

Creer, K.M., "Symposium on Palaeomagnetism and Secular Variation," *Geophysical Jour.,* v. 1, 1958, pp. 99-105.

Davis, G.H., and others. "Land Subsidence, Related to Decline of Artesian Head in the Ocala Limestone at Savannah, Georgia," *Bull. Geol. Soc. Amer.,* v. 70, 1959, p. 1585.

Dewar, D., "Recent Theories of the Origin of Man," *Victoria Inst., J. Tr.,* v. 86, 1954, pp. 1-16; disc., pp. 83-91.

Dirac, P.A.M. "Fixation of Coordinates in the Hamiltonian Theory of Gravitation," *Phys. Rev.,* v. 114, 1959, pp. 924-930.

Drake, C.L., and others. "Continental Margins and Geosynclines, East Coast of North America North of Cape Hatteras," *Bull. Geol. Soc. America,* v. 68, 1957, pp. 1718-19.

Dunbar, C.O. *Historical Geology.* New York: John Wiley and Sons, 1949, 567 pp.

Elsasser, W.M., and Munk, W. "Geomagnetic Drift and the Rotation of the Earth," pp. 228-236, *in* Benihoff, H., et al., editors, "Contributions in Geophysics in Honor of Beno Gutenberg," Pergamon Press, 1958, 224 pp.

Emiliani, C. "Pleistocene Temperatures," *Jour. Geology,* v. 63, 1955, pp. 538-578.

———————— "Oligocene and Miocene Temperatures of the Equatorial and Sub-tropical Atlantic Ocean," *Jour. Geology,* v. 64, 1956, pp. 281-288.

———————— "Paleotemperature Analysis of Core 280 and Pleistocene Correlations," *Jour. Geology,* v. 66, 1958, pp. 264-275.

Ericson, D.B., and others. "Late-Pleistocene Climates and Deep-sea Sediments," *Science,* v. 124, 1956, pp. 385-389.

Ewing, M., and Donn, W.L. "A Theory of Ice Ages II," *Science,* v. 127, 1958, pp. 1159-1162.

Furth, H.P. "High Magnetic Field Research," *Science,* v. 132, 1960, pp. 387-393.

Gidley, J.W. "Notice of the Occurrence of a Pleistocene Camel North of the Arctic Circle," *Smithsonian Misc. Coll.,* v. 60, pub. no. 2173.

Gold, T. "Instability of the Earth's Axis of Rotation," *Nature,* v. 175, 1955, pp. 526-529; disc. by Goodhart and Thomas, v. 176, p. 349.

Goldberg, E.D., and Koide, M. "Ionium-Thorium Chronology in Deep-sea Sediments of the Pacific," *Science,* v. 128, 1958, p. 1003.

Gross, H. "Die Fortschritte der Radiokarbon-Methode 1952-1956," *Eiszeitalter u. Gegenwart,* v. 8, 1957, pp. 141-180.

Heck, N.H. "List of Seismic Sea Waves," *Bull. Seismol. Soc. Amer.,* v. 37, no. 4, 1947, pp. 269-286.

Heezen, B.C., and Tharp, Marie. "Physiographic Diagram of the North Atlantic," *Geol. Soc. America Spec. Paper 65* (pt. 1), 1958. Available from the Geological Society of America, 419 W. 117 Street, New York, N.Y.

Heiskanen, W.A., and Vening Meisnesz, F.A. *The Earth and Its Gravity Field.* New York: McGraw-Hill, 1958, 470 pp.

Hough, J. "Pleistocene Lithology of Antarctic Ocean Bottom Sediments," *Jour. Geology,* v. 58, 1950, p. 257.

———————— "Pacific Climate Record in a Pacific Ocean Core Sample," *Jour. Geol.,* v. 61, 1953, pp. 252-262.

Iida, K., and Wada, T. "Vertical Earth Movement Around the Bay of Ise as Deduced from Changes in Heights of Mean Sea Levels," Nagoya Univ., *J. Earth Sci.,* v. 3, 1955, pp. 91-104.

India Meteorological Dept., Calcutta: India Weather Review, 1926, 311 pp.

Ishii, I. "On the Submerged Forest of Uozu and the Subsidence of the Ground," *Jour. Geog.,* Tokyo, v. 64, 1955, pp. 33-43.

Kolbe, R.W. "Fresh-water Diatoms from Atlantic Deep-sea Sediments," *Science,* v. 126, 1957, pp. 1053-1056.

———————— "Turbidity Currents and Displaced Fresh-water

Diatoms," *Science,* v. 127, 1958; p. 1504.

Lipson, J. "Potassium-argon Dating of Sedimentary Rocks," *Bull. Geol. Soc. America,* v. 69, 1958, pp. 137-150.

Longwell, C.R., Knopf, A., and Flint, R.F. *A Textbook of Geology, Part I—Physical Geology.* New York: Wiley, 1939, 543 pp.

Mellis, O. "Sedimentation in the Romanche Deep (A Contribution to the Explanation of the Genesis of the Deep-sea Sands in the Atlantic Ocean)," *Geol. Rundschau,* v. 47, no. 1, 1956, pp. 218-234; translation in Int. Geol. Rev., v. 1, no. 9, pp. 50-58.

Menard, H.W., and Fisher, R.L. "Clipperton Fracture Zone in the Northeast Equatorial Pacific," *Jour. Geology,* v. 66, 1958, pp. 239-253.

Menard, H.W. "Development of Median Elevations in Ocean Basins," *Bull. Geol. Soc. America,* v. 69, 1958, pp. 1179-1186.

Miyabe, N. "Vertical Earth Movements in Japan Deduced from Results of Relevelings," *Pacific Sci.,* Cong. 7th, New Zealand, Pr. v. 2, 1953, pp. 262-263.

Momose, Kan-Ichi. "Paleomagnetic Researches for the Pliocene Volcanic Rocks in Central Japan (1)," *Jour. Geomagnetism and Geoelect.,* v. 10, no. 1, 1958, pp. 12-19, 1 fig., 2 tables.

Opdyke, N.D., and Runcorn, S.K. "New Evidence for Reversal of the Geomagnetic Field near the Pliocene-Pleistocene Boundary," *Science,* v. 123, no. 3208, 1956, pp. 1126-1127.

Ottman, F., and Picard, J. "Sur Quelques Mouvements Tectoniques Récents sur les Côtes Nord et est de la Sicile," *Acad. Sci.,* Paris, C.R. t. 239, no. 19, 1954, pp. 1230-1231.

Pettersson, H. "Radioactivity and the Chronology of the Ocean Floor," *in* Faul, H., *Nuclear Geology,* New York: Wiley, 1954, 414 pp.

Plass, G.N. "Carbon Dioxide and the Climate," *Amer. Scientist,* v. 44, 1956, pp. 302-316.

Richter, C.F. *Elementary Seismology.* San Francisco: Freeman, 1958, 768 pp.

_____ "Seismic Regionalization," *Bull. Seis. Soc. America,* v. 49, no. 2, 1959, pp. 123-162, 7 figs.

Rigey, J.K., and Burckle, L.H. "Turbidity Currents and Displaced Fresh-water Diatoms," *Science,* v. 127, 1958, p. 1504.

Runcorn, S.K. "Paleomagnetic Survey in Arizona and Utah: Preliminary Results," *Bull. Geol. Soc. America,* v. 67, 1956, pp. 301-316.

_____ "Paleomagnetic Comparisons Between Europe and North America," *Geol. Assoc. Canada,* v. 8, 1956 b, pp. 77-85.

_____ *Methods and Techniques in Geophysics,* Interscience Pub. Inc., New York, 1960, 374 pp.

Sears, P.B., and others. "Palynology in Southern North America, Pt. IV: Pleistocene Climate in Mexico," *Bull. Geol. Soc. America,* v. 66, 1955, pp. 521-530.

de Terra, H. "New Approach to the Problem of Man's Origin," *Science,* v. 124, 1956, pp. 1282-1286.

Tillotson, E. "Notes on the Agadir Disaster," *Nature,* v. 186, 1960, p. 199.

Tomascheck, R. "Earthquakes and Uranus: Misuse of a Statistical Test of Significance," *Nature,* v. 186, 1960, p. 338.

Umbgrove, J.H. *Pulse of the Earth.* The Hague: Martinus Nijhoff, 1947.

U.S. Bureau of the Census. *Statistical Abstract of the United States,* 18th ed., Washington, 1959.

U.S. Coast and Geodetic Survey. "Earthquake History of California and Western Nevada, Part II—Stronger Earthquakes of California and Western Nevada," Serial No. 609, Washington, 1951, 35 pp.

U.S. Weather Bureau. *Monthly Weather Review,* v. 54, no. 10 (October, 1926). pp. 409-452.

Weber, J. "Detection and Generation of Gravitational Waves," *Physical Rev.,* v. 117, 1959, pp. 306-313.

Wollard, G.P. "Areas of Tectonic Activity in the United States as Indicated by Earthquake Epicenters," *Trans. Amer. Geophys. Union,* v. 39, no. 6, 1958, pp. 1135-1150.

Wood, H.O., and Neumann, F. "Modified Mercalli Intensity Scale of 1931," *Bull. Seism. Soc. Amer.,* v. 21, 1931, pp. 277-283.

Worzel, J.L., and others. "Gravity Observations at Sea. Pt. 1: The Bahama Islands Region: (Abstract)," *Bull. Geol. Soc. Amer.,* 1953, p. 1494.

APPENDIX

The Psychic Viewpoint

The foregoing comparative study raises several questions, with reference to earth changes predicted for the 40-year period from 1958 to 1998. The three most critical questions that come to this author's mind follow, and answers that are based upon information found in the readings are also presented, for the reader's consideration.

Will the predicted earth changes really come to pass?

This question was very probably a burning one in the mind of the psychic through whom the predictions came. It is understandable, therefore, that Mr. Cayce might dream about "his" prophecies—about their meaning and about their veracity. On the night of March 3, 1936, while returning to Virginia Beach from Detroit by train, Edgar Cayce had the following dream:

"He had been born again in 2100 A.D. in Nebraska. The sea apparently covered all of the western part of the country, as the city where he lived was on the coast. The family name was a strange one. At an early age as a child he declared himself to be Edgar Cayce who had lived two hundred years before.

"Scientists, men with long beards, little hair, and thick glasses were called in to observe the child. They decided to visit the places where he said he had been born, lived, and worked— in Kentucky, Alabama, New York, Michigan, and Virginia. Taking the child with them the group of scientists visited these places in a long, cigar-shaped, metal flying ship which moved at high speed.

"Water covered part of Alabama. Norfolk, Virginia, had become an immense seaport. New York had been destroyed either by war or an earthquake and was being rebuilt. Industries were scattered over the countryside. Most of the houses were of glass.

"Many records of Edgar Cayce's work were discovered and collected. The group returned to Nebraska, taking the records with them for study."

On June 30, 1936, a reading was given in which an interpretation of Mr. Cayce's dream-experience was requested. The answer follows:

These experiences, as has oft been indicated, come to the body in those manners in which there may be help, strength, for periods when doubt or fear may have arisen. As in this experience, there were about the entity those influences which appeared to make for such a record of confusion as to appear to the material, or mental-minded as a doubting or fearing of those sources that made for [caused] the periods through which the entity was passing in that particular period.

And the vision was that there might be strength, that there might be an understanding, that though the moment may appear dark, though there may be periods of misinterpreting of purposes, even *these* will be turned into that which will be the very proof itself in the experiences of the entity and those whom the entity might, whom the entity would, in its experience through the earth plane, help; and those to whom the entity might give hope and understanding.

This then is the interpretation. As has been given, "Fear not." Keep the faith; for those that be with thee are greater than those that would hinder. Though the very heavens fall, though the earth shall be changed, though the heavens shall pass, the promises in Him are sure and will stand—as in that day—as the proof of thy activity in the lives and hearts of thy fellow men.

For indeed and in truth ye know, "As ye do it unto thy fellow man, ye do it unto thy God, to thyself." For, with *self* effaced, God may indeed glorify thee and make thee *stand* as one who is called for a purpose in the dealings, in the relationships with thy fellow man.

Be not unmindful that He is nigh unto thee in every trial, in every temptation, and hath not willed that thou shouldst perish.

Make thy will, then, one with His. Be not afraid.

That is the interpretation. That the periods from the material angle as visioned are to come to pass matters not to the soul but do thy duty *today! Tomorrow* will care for itself.

These changes in the earth will come to pass, for the time and times and half times are at an end[9] and there begin these

9. "...where she [Earth] is nourished for a time, and times, and half a time..." (Rev. 12:14) "...until a time and times and the dividing of time" (Dan. 7:25) "...it *shall* BE for a time, times, and a half...all these *things* shall be finished." (Dan. 12:7)

periods for the readjustments. For how hath He given? "The righteous shall inherit the earth."

Hast thou, my brethren, a heritage in the earth?

294-185, June 30, 1936

The above reading is the best that the author could find in the way of a direct answer to this first question, without drawing upon those predictions already cited, that have actually come to pass. As to the actual form that these earth changes might take, and as to their timing, the following excerpts may be worthy of consideration:

Q-15. What form will they take?
A-15. To be sure, that may depend upon much that deals with the metaphysical, as well as to that people called actual, or in truth! for as understood—or should be [understood] by the entity—there are those conditions that in the activity of individuals, in line of thought and endeavor, oft keep many a city and many a land intact through their application of the spiritual laws in their associations *with* individuals. . .

311-10, November 19, 1932

As to times [of earth changes], as to seasons, as to places, *alone* is it given to those who have named the name—and who bear the mark of those of His calling and His election in their bodies. To them it shall be given. 3976-15, January 19, 1934

Q-13. When is this likely to occur?
A-13. As to times and places and seasons, as it has indeed been indicated in the greater relationships that have been established by the prophets and sages of old—and especially as given by Him, "As to the day and the hour, who knoweth? *No one,* save the Creative Forces." 416-7, October 7, 1935

Q-3. What can we do to counteract such serious happenings?
A-3. Make known the trouble—*where it lies; that they who have forgotten God must right about face!*

3976-26, April 28, 1941

Tendencies in the hearts and souls of men are such that these [upheavals] may be brought about. For, as indicated through these channels oft, it is not the world, the earth, the environs about it nor the planetary influences, nor the associations or activities, that *rule* man. *Rather* does man—by *his* compliance with divine law—bring *order* out of chaos; or, by his *disregard* of the associations and laws of divine influence, bring chaos and *destructive* forces into his experience.

For *He* hath given, "Though the heavens and the earth pass away, my *word* shall *not* pass away!" This is oft considered as just a beautiful saying, or something to awe those who have been stirred by some experience. But applying them into the conditions that exist in the affairs of the world and the universe in the present, what *holds* them—what are the foundations of the earth? The word of the Lord!

416-7, October 7, 1935

How should we regard those changes that do come about?

What is needed most in the earth today? That the sons of men be warned that the day of the Lord is near at hand, and that those who have been and are unfaithful must meet themselves in those things which come to pass in their experience.

5148-2, May 29, 1944

Q-3. What is meant by "the day of the Lord is near at hand"?
A-3. That as has been promised through the prophets and the sages of old, the time—and half time—has been and is being fulfilled in this day and generation, and that soon there will again appear in the earth that one through whom many will be called to meet those that are preparing the way for His day in the earth. The Lord, then, will come, "even as ye have seen him go."
Q-4. How soon?
A-4. When those that are His have made the way clear, *passable,* for Him to come.   262-49, July 9, 1933

Don't think that there will not be trouble, but those who put their trust wholly in the Lord will not come up missing but will find conditions, circumstances, activities, someway and somehow much to be thankful for.   1467-18, April 10, 1944

Perhaps this last question might better have been worded, "How ought we to regard adversity in general?" Consider the following:

These experiences then that have shattered hopes, that have brought disappointments, that have produced periods when there seemed little or nothing left in material life—if they are used in the experiences as stepping-stones and not as those things that bring resentments, accusations to others, those influences that create discontent, we will find they will become helpful experiences that may guide the entity, the bodily influences into a haven that is quiet and peaceful.

Hence the necessity as is in the entity's whole experience that the faith, the hope in a divinity that is *within* be held—[a divinity] that shapes the destinies of individual experiences in such a way that the opportunities that come into the lives of individuals are those things which if taken correctly make for the greater soul development.

. . .look not back. . .upon those shadows of doubt and fear that bring so oft so much discouragement that one fails to know there is a Friend indeed that is mindful of *every* thought, act and deed of a soul. And He hath not willed that any should be fraught with the fears of despair, but hath, with each temptation, with each doubt and fear prepared a way of escape; that those who remain faithful will come to know the way in a much more glorious manner.

1300-1, November 28, 1936

The Scientific Viewpoint

In this appendix to an article which purports to make a comparison between psychic and scientific information, it seems appropriate to cite a few passages that give an indication of the sort of scientific evaluation that one might expect of the questions raised in this study. (The views cited do not necessarily reflect the views of all scientists.)

Fundamental to the evaluation is the "scientific" view of psychic phenomena in general—taking the definition of psychic phenomena to mean *activity of the soul force*. In other words, what is the scientific viewpoint of the concept of a soul in every human being? In an article in the August 1, 1960, issue of *Time* magazine, the biologist Julian Huxley is quoted as saying, or cited as believing, that (p. 45):

Theology is based on "a combination of an elaborate god-theory with a subsidiary but equally elaborate soul-theory," and is limited in applicability and the power of self-correction. Humanism, on the other hand, is "acquiring a well-organized theoretical basis in the form of a comprehensive theory of evolution as a whole"; it is capable of unlimited development, and "its reliance on scientific method" instead of divine intervention and revelation "makes it automatically self-correcting."

God and the soul are hypotheses; so were evolution and the atom, but these two are now theories "with high predictive value and practical applicability." Whereas "the soul-hypothesis, after being promoted by the scholastic theologians to the dignity of high theory, is now increasingly failing to account for psychological and neurological facts: the soul as an entity is disappearing."

Thus, if the soul is a myth, then so are psychic manifestations myths, for "psychic" is "of the soul."

With reference to all theories about sunken continents, the January, 1960, *Cosmopolitan Magazine* quotes this scientific viewpoint:

"None of them is right," says Dr. Bruce Heezen, a highly respected oceanographer at Columbia University's world-renowned Lamont Geological Observatory. "There was no Atlantis. The books and papers on Atlantis are essentially fiction. Fascinating fiction, but fiction nevertheless.

"Eleven thousand years ago the ocean level all around the world was perhaps three hundred feet lower than it is today. The eastern coastline of our United States, for instance, was some one hundred miles farther out in the Atlantic Ocean in that bygone era.

"Then suddenly, about eleven thousand years ago, the Ice Age was over. The ice caps receded dramatically, and billions of gallons of ice and snow poured into the sea. The result was a dramatic, sudden, and terrifying rising of the sea level all around the world—an inundation which we have verified by half a dozen different types of research available to us today. The rise undoubtedly caused the flooding of many low-level seaside communities where primitive man had chosen to build his early towns and cities.

"Atlantis, I am sure, is the legendary name of some such coastal town in Africa or Europe which died a swift, horrible death in the rising sea.

"Mu, Lemuria, the Portuguese 'Green Island,' the Breton city of Is—these drowned cultures, too, were probably inundated by the same rising sea, because every inch of shoreline on every continent in this era felt the terrible impact of the ocean's rise.

"But a real lost continent called Atlantis? No, I'm afraid not."

Finally, in the April 1, 1960, issue of *Science,* there appears (p. 974) what is perhaps a fair statement of the scientist's solution to the future problems that confront humanity. The quote is from Prof. G.G. Simpson's *The World into Which Darwin Led Us:*

"In the post-Darwinian world another answer seems fairly

clear: man is responsible to himself and for himself. 'Himself' here means the whole human species, not only the individual and certainly not just those of a certain color of hair or cast of features.

"The fact that man knows that he evolves entails the possibility that he can do something to influence his own biological destiny.

"The fact that uncontrolled evolution often leads to degeneration and usually to extinction makes it highly advisable that man take a hand in determining his own future evolution. If man proceeds on the wrong evolutionary assumptions—for instance, on those of Neo-Lamarckism or Michurinism—whatever he does is sure to be wrong. If he proceeds on the right assumptions, what he does may still be wrong, but at least it has a chance of being right.

"A world in which man must rely on himself, in which he is not the darling of the gods but only another, albeit extraordinary, aspect of nature, is by no means congenial to the immature or the wishful thinkers. That is plainly a major reason why even now, a hundred years after *The Origin of Species,* most people have not really entered the world into which Darwin led—alas!—only a minority of us. Life may conceivably be happier for some people in the older worlds of superstition. It is possible that some children are made happy by a belief in Santa Claus, but adults should prefer to live in a world of reality and reason.

"Perhaps I should end on that note of mere preference, but it is impossible to do so. It is a characteristic of this world to which Darwin opened the door that unless *most* of us do enter it and live maturely and rationally in it, the future of mankind is dim, indeed—if there is any future."

Scale of Earthquake Disturbance

The following description of effects at grades VI-IX of the Modified Mercalli scale (M.M.) of 1931 is a partial extraction from the original publication. (Wood and Neumann, 1931) Marginal notes in brackets are the approximate equivalents on the older Rossi-Forel scale (R.F.), according to Richter. (1959, p. 158) A suggested rewording of the M.M. scale, with comments and discussion, is given by Richter. (1958, pp. 136-139, 650-652)

VI [VI-VII R.F.]

Felt by all, indoors and outdoors. Awakened all. Persons made to move unsteadily. Liquid set in strong motion. Fall of plaster in small amount. Cracked plaster and chimneys somewhat.

VII

Frightened all; general alarm, all ran outdoors. Noticed by persons driving cars. Some found it difficult to stand. Trees and bushes shaken moderately. Water turbid from mud stirred up. Rang large church bells. Suspended objects made to quiver.

[VIII R.F.]

Damage negligible in buildings of good construction, slight to moderate in buildings that are well built, considerable in poorly built or badly designed structures. Fall of plaster in large amount, also stucco. Fall of cornices from large buildings and high towers. Broke numerous windows; cracked chimneys and walls.

VIII

Fright general; alarm approaches panic. Disturbed persons driving cars. Trees shaken strongly. Changes, permanent and temporary, in flow of springs and wells.

[VIII+ to IX R.F.]

Damage slight in structures built especially to withstand earthquakes; considerable in ordinary substantial buildings, partial collapse. Fall of walls. Twisting fall of chimneys, monuments, towers. Moved heavy furniture.

IX [IX+ R.F.]

Panic general. Cracked ground conspiciously. Damage considerable in masonry structures especially built; great in substantial masonry buildings, some collapse in large part; wholly shifted frame buildings off foundations.

EARTH CHANGES ADDENDUM[1]

Seven years have passed since new material was last added to this study of earth changes predicted in the Edgar Cayce readings. In the intervening time there have been no geological events, with the possible exception of the 1964 Alaskan quake, which could be said to represent clear fulfillment of the Cayce prophecies of dramatic crustal changes over wide areas for the period 1958 through 1998. Certain social developments have occurred, however, which suggest that the world may be on the brink of events that the readings implied were either strong probabilities or inevitable occurrences for this critical 40-year period.

Strife

Among the social developments that the readings on page 96 implied were strong probabilities are two: increased strife between capital and labor, and a social division in America. The "division" prophesied has for many years been interpreted by students as one that could arise out of racial inharmonies. Reading 3976-24 indicated that this division would be apparent *before* the death in office of the second of two presidents "that next" would not live through their office. The president at the time of the reading was Franklin D. Roosevelt, and it is this author's opinion that John F. Kennedy was only the first of two presidents who would die in office, *next* after Roosevelt. The death of the "second of the presidents" and the "division" in America are linked in this reading to "a mob rule."

It is clear that since 1939, the year of the reading, strife between capital and labor has been increasing. Racial strife also has grown stronger in the last few years, and at the present the Black Power advocates are striving for separate white and black societies—in essence, a divided America. One president since Roosevelt has died in office, and at this writing the nation seems to be *expecting* another summer of intensified racial strife, with attendant mob violence. The widely publicized

---

1. Manuscript received March 26, 1968.

predictions of strife by various study commissions on racial disorders seems destined to become self-fulfilling prophecies.

At this point it is instructive to shift to a consideration of the reading on page 85 that refers to the possible submergence of portions of Alabama, beginning in "thirty-six to thirty-eight." With the prediction is the caution, the activities and thoughts of individuals can "keep many a city and many a land intact." The corollary is that by unrighteous thoughts and acts many a city or land may be adversely affected by crustal movements in the critical 40-year period in which we are now living.

Some students of the Cayce data on earth changes believe that the Alabama prophecy was erroneous because crustal movements there have not yet become apparent. The reading (p. 85) clearly states, however, that the physical changes would not begin to be apparent "for some period yet." They were only to begin (in a subtle fashion) in "thirty-six to thirty-eight," presumably as a result of the upheavals in the interior of the earth mentioned on page 84. Information in 1152-11 (p. 93) on the submergence of portions of Carolina and Georgia is in the same category as the one on Alabama.

It would seem that the hope of future days will lie in man's understanding that "there are those conditions that in the activity of individuals, in line of thought and endeavor, keep oft many a city and many a land intact through their application of the spiritual laws in their associations with individuals." (311-10, November 19, 1932)

Thus, social developments of the last eight years have increased the probability that the readings just mentioned may turn out to be correct. What then of some of the other prophecies of the foregoing text?

Anti-gravity

A reading (p. 86) given in 1932 predicted that the forces in nature "as make for iron to swim" would be discovered, in 1958, to be usable for the movement of heavy objects. The reading indicated that "stone floats in the air in the same manner," and that this principle, which might be electromagnetic propulsion, was used in the construction of the Great Pyramid of Gizeh.

At the time of the last augmentation of this booklet, the author was unaware of the work that had been done by Dr. Stuart Way, of the Westinghouse Research Laboratories, on electromagnetic propulsion. In a Westinghouse memorandum

113

dated October 15, 1958, Dr. Way reported on his theoretical examination of the use of bipolar electric and magnetic fields for the propulsion of a submarine. His discovery was made before the potentialities of super-conducting magnets were known. By 1965, technology was sufficiently advanced to permit him to circulate a paper (1) entitled, "Propulsion of Submarines by Lorentz Forces in the Surrounding Sea." On July 21, 1966, he supervised the launching, at Goleta, California, of a 10-foot-long model submarine that ran successfully for 12 minutes at a speed of 1.5 knots, by electromagnetic propulsion alone.

Whether it was also discovered in 1958 that stone can be made to float in air, by the application of electromagnetic forces, is presently unknown. Perhaps the reading only meant to imply that the technology for the movement of stone by electromagnetic forces would *follow* from a discovery like that made by Dr. Way in 1958.

Upheavals in Western America

In the reading on page 87, there appears the rather unequivocal statement that "the earth will be broken up in the western portion of America," during the 1958 to 1998 period. At this writing (March, 1968), the world's last *great* quake (above 8.0 on the Richter scale) was the Alaskan quake on March 27, 1964, in which the earth's crust was fractured and displaced both upward and downward over an area of about 310,000 square miles. By now, seismologists are talking about a "great quake holiday," because this has been the longest period without the occurrence of a great earthquake since the beginning of systematic recordings of earthquakes some 70 years ago. There also has been a large drop-off in the number of *major* quakes (7.0 to 7.9 Richter scale) and, although seismologists are not in agreement as to the cause of this drop-off, most are concerned about its implications.

A similar period of relative quiet in 1954-1956 ended with 27 major and two great quakes in 1957. Over 4,000 deaths and millions of dollars of damage were caused in several countries and the state of Hawaii.

It would seem that the Alaskan upheaval, the constant references by renowned seismologists to the fact that California is long overdue for a great quake, and the implications of a pending break in the earthquake "holiday" make a foreboding pattern, as far as western America is concerned. One would hope that the inhabitants of western America could so live that this area would not have to experience a "breaking up," in spite of the matter-of-fact prophecy of the reading.

Turmoil, Earth Changes, Hunger, and "Safety Lands"

A reading not appearing in *Earth Changes* specifies Norfolk, Virginia, as belonging to one of the "safety lands" for the 1958-1998 period. This city may be added to the list of specific places, such as "portions of what is now Ohio, Indiana, and Illinois and much of the southern portion of Canada," and "Virginia Beach or the area," referred to on pages 91 and 93, as safe areas when turmoils and crustal movements are prophesied to occur. The reading states:

**Q-1. *In view of the uncertainty of existing conditions, did I act wisely in establishing my home in Norfolk?*
A-1. It's a mighty good place, and a safe place when turmoils are to arise, though it may appear that it may be in the line of those areas to rise, while many a higher land will sink. This is a good area to stick to.   2746-2, December 11, 1943**

In 1943 a New York resident asked, "Is the farm purchase suggested still advisable for the region between Washington and Norfolk?"
The answer was:

**These conditions have not changed. For the hardships for this country have not begun yet, so far as the supply and demand for foods are concerned.
257-254, December 18, 1943**

These and other readings suggest that the entire area of Tidewater Virginia, from Virginia Beach on the east, to near Richmond on the west and Washington on the north, will be a safety land in terms of crustal movements. But the matter of obtaining sufficient foods will be with the residents nonetheless.

Anyone who can buy a farm is fortunate and buy it if you don't want to grow something and don't want to grow hungry in some days to come.   3620-1, January 27, 1944

Certainly, turmoil and strife can profoundly affect the supply and distribution of food; so could the earth changes prophesied in the Cayce readings. The question of large-scale crustal movements as a part of the earth's "experience" bears upon the readings that predicted the rising of "lost Atlantis" in 1968 and 1969. In reading 1602-3, the question was asked about Atlantis rising, as prophesied by Jacob Boehme 300 years ago, in relation to a nearly identical prophecy in the readings. This prophecy referred to "the cycle of the solar activity" and the change between the Piscean and Aquarian ages. It finished with, "This is a gradual, not a cataclysmic activity in the experience of the earth in this period." The author discovered this reading only three years ago. It seems to imply that relatively gradual crustal deformations may characterize the 1968-1969 period, but that these will be relatively mild in their destructive effects only by comparison to some of the other truly cataclysmic episodes in the earth's previous experience.

ATLANTIS AT BIMINI?

One of the late Edgar Cayce's more startling prophecies was that in 1968 and 1969 remains of Atlantis would rise from the sea, in and near the Bimini Islands. (Fig. A1) What evidence is there for the credibility of such predictions?

The Cayce data first pinpointed the Bimini Islands as containing the most accessible remains of "the Atlantean civilization," and the first reading in the series was given at the request of a group of men seeking oil and buried treasure at Bimini. Present were the conductor of the reading, Dr. T.B. House; Edgar Cayce's stenographer, Gladys Davis Turner; and one of the group requesting information.

Dr. House: You will give a reading on Bimini Island, located in the Atlantic Ocean, about 45 miles almost due east of Miami, Dade County, Florida. You will go over this island and tell us whether there is oil on this island in sufficient quantities to insure profit. If so, give us the log of the formations that would be gone through in drilling to the oil sand and depth of the well necessary to reach the oil production, and also tell us if there are any treasures buried on this island. If so, when were they buried, and where can they be located, and to whom do they belong at this time?

Mr. Cayce: Yes, we have the land known as Bimini, in the Atlantic Ocean. In the formation of the land, we find this of the nature that would make the oil production very low, for this is of the coral structure in the greater part, but this is the highest portion left above the waves of a once great continent, upon which the civilization as now exists in the world's history found much of that as would be used as means for attaining that civilization.　　　　　　　　**996-1, August 14, 1926**

The remainder of this first reading speaks of treasures buried at Bimini and gives instructions for finding the most valuable of them. The next six readings are missing from the vault of the Edgar Cayce Foundation. The eighth to eleventh readings deal with the failure of the group to find a treasure on Bimini. The twelfth and final reading in the series refers to a "project" for developing the Bimini Islands into a great tourist resort. The project had apparently been the subject of the missing readings. The last reading was given in Miami's Halcyon Hotel.

Mrs. Cayce: You will have before you the islands of North and South Bimini, and the submerged land adjacent to same. You will outline in detail the necessary procedure to finance and develop this project, in the way of building streets, sidewalks, sea walls, canals, harbors, sewerage, water and electrical system, ice plant, laundries, and everything necessary to complete a resort city. You will answer all questions which I will ask you regarding this.

Mr. Cayce: Yes, we have the islands as are seen in the natural formations as are visible at the present time.

Now, we find there are many things that may be said as respecting the plausibility and the advisability of making a resort city in this location. First we would give, this would not be near as large an undertaking as it appears on the face of conditions, for this may be stored away as truth for those that would go about to accomplish such conditions: There will be found many, many, *many* sources of revenue for those undertaking such a project, for these mountain tops— especially that along the north and eastern shores of the north and northern portion of the south island—will produce many various minerals and various other conditions that will be remunerative when the projects are undertaken; and well that the ones that do such labors—as the dredging as necessary, the building as necessary, the walls, etc.—be followed close in their operations, for these will uncover many various conditions that may be turned into dollars—and dollars—and dollars!
                                                    996-12, March 2, 1927

Several paragraphs at this point in the reading explain how the reclamation of land should be undertaken and how financing might be obtained. The reading continues:

This [inlet between north and south Bimini] also lends to the modes of manufacture—of electro-hydro power in the waves, if necessary, by the tides—such as have been and are being builded in the Bay of Fundy—for with the walls as may be built in the western coasts of the inlet—that may be closed or left open, or builded for the purpose of an inland sea for the boat, the port and for the fishing, bathing and the like—this may be builded in such a manner on the northern shore of the south, and the southern shore of the north island, as to facilitate the power sufficient to electrify the whole of the lands that may be acclaimed and reclaimed. 996-12

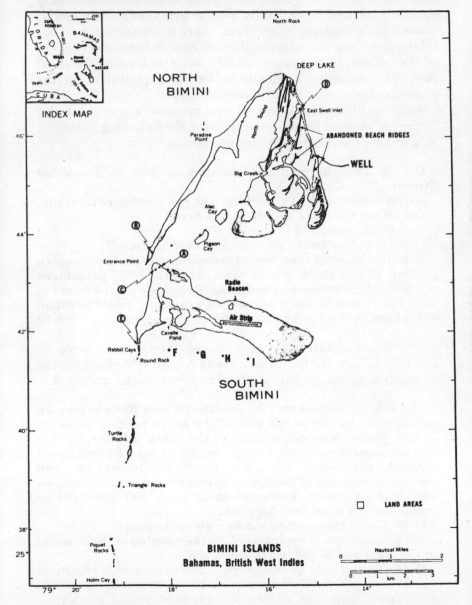

Figure A1—Map of Bimini Islands showing drilling sites and features referred to in text.

The walls just mentioned would be located across the inlet at entrance point. (Fig. A1) Strong tidal currents in this inlet lend credence to the suggestion that the inlet be dammed to make a hydro-electric plant. Currents range up to 4.0 knots at times of spring tides, and there is only a short period of slack water at times of tide change. In addition, there is an asymmetry to the tidal-current curve such that the ebb flow, to the southwest out of the lagoon, lasts approximately twice as long as the flood flow. This situation is ideally suited for exploitation for the purpose of generating hydro-electric power.

After additional information was provided about obtaining financial backing for the resort project, the following questions and answers were recorded by the stenographer:

Q-1. Is this the continent known as Alta or Poseidia? *[Atlantis]*
A-1. A temple of the Poseidians was in a portion of this land.
Q-2. What minerals will be found here?
A-2. Gold, spar, and icthyolite [?]
Q-3. How deep in the ground will that be found?
A-3. In the wall that would be builded from the western portion of the south island towards that of the *prominent* portions of the southern portion of isle—these will be found in the 12 to 15 foot levels. The *vein,* as workable, would be found extending in the northeast southwest direction. . .   996-12

Additional questions were asked about the project's financing. Then the information was volunteered about the use of sulphur waters on the north island for healing purposes.

The sulphur waters may be obtained where there is seen an old channel on the north end of the south portion of north island. These, we find, will be of the black sulphur, yet for certain conditions—and for the baths as may be instituted through same—will be quite beneficial to health, and especially to those of the neurotic conditions—nervousness—and of the germ of rheumatic conditions, see? This will be found only 89 to 90 feet deep, see?
Q-16. Could this port be made a shipping port?
A-16. Be made a shipping port, by the opening of the channel to the west and to the north here, see?
Q-17. What would be the proper way to open this channel?
A-17. See, when a channel is made here—as we see, the sands only come from the southern end, that would hinder or produce a bar. When dredges are made, only the extension of

these obstructions—that only divert the channel—which is of moving waters—to the outer edge, would prevent and keep the bar from being moved back and forth across. Rocks or piles, see? along this end.   996-12

A final paragraph of advice ends this initial series of readings on Bimini.

The next reference to Atlantean remains in the vicinity of Bimini came in a series of 13 rather lengthy readings, given in 1932, on the lost continent of Atlantis. It ends with the words:

The British West Indies or the Bahamas, and a portion of same that may be seen in the present—if the geological survey would be made in some of these—especially, or notably, in Bimini and in the Gulf Stream through this vicinity these may be even yet determined.   364-3, February 16, 1932

The final references to Atlantean remains at Bimini occur in readings 587-4, 5750-1, and 958-3, that discuss a well at Bimini, archaeological remains there, and the rising of a "Poseidian" temple in 1968 and 1969. These references are also discussed elsewhere (1).

General Credibility of Bimini Readings

In reviewing the geological information in the Bimini readings, one notes that the psychic source held out little hope for oil production at Bimini, because the subsurface formations were "of the coral structure in the greater part." Although coralline strata do not preclude entirely the presence of producing horizons, it is probable that little in the way of significant production would be obtained from the strata underlying Bimini in light of the failure of a test well at nearby Andros Island, on the opposite side of the Great Bahama Bank. Recent scientific opinion holds that the northwestern Bahama Banks are formed exclusively of coral and other carbonate rocks, quite probably to depths of 4,000 feet (2) and possibly to depths of 15,000 feet. According to Newell and Rigby (3), for example:

"The character of the rocks beneath the Andros platform, as shown by a deep boring, indicates more or less continuous deposition of calcareous sediments during subsidence since the early Cretaceous period. The deepest boring (about 14,800 ft.) made in the Bahamas thus far was made as a petroleum prospect by the Superior Oil Company, and others. . .on Stafford Creek, Andros Island. This hole penetrated only carbonate rocks."

These authors also give details of a 400-foot exploratory borehole that was put down six miles south of the city of Nassau (Fig. A1), which also penetrated exclusively carbonate rocks. To the north of Bimini, at Hawksbill Creek on the southwestern shore of Grand Bahama Island, Harrison (4) studied 73 borings that penetrated carbonate rocks exclusively to depths of 40 to 70 feet below tide. A test well drilled about 100 miles to the west of Bimini penetrated 14,000 feet of carbonate rock.

Thus, there is general confirmation of the psychic data, as to the nature of "the greater part" of the rocks underlying Bimini. Attention is turned to the statement ". . .for these mountain tops—especially that along the north and eastern shores of the north and northern portion of the south island—will produce many various minerals, and various other conditions. . ." (996-12) The implication is that mountain peaks lie beneath certain parts of north and south Bimini. A problem immediately arises. Would these peaks be composed of carbonate rock, as one would infer from the earlier psychic reference to the subsurface being "of the coral structure *in the greater part*," or would the mountains be coral-covered peaks of igneous or metamorphic rock that, logically, could "produce many various minerals"? Again, what credibility is there to the idea of mountaintops underlying the Bimini Islands in the first place?

Extrapolation of recent seismic-refraction results by R.E. Sheridan (5) suggests a depth to the igneous or metamorphic basement rock beneath the Bimini Islands of the order of six kilometers or more. Because the seismic velocities of crystalline basement can be similar to that of high-velocity crystalline limestone, however, and because the Banks are an area of carbonate facies, estimates of depths to the igneous or metamorphic-rock basement can be made only with difficulty.

The morphology of the basement rock complex in the northwest Bahamas was assumed by Hess (2) to be similar to that of the southern Appalachians, but exhibiting subdued valley-and-ridge topography that trended parallel to the trend of the deep channels that are incised into the Banks. In 1947, a total-intensity aeromagnetic survey was made of the Bahamas for several oil companies by Aero Services Corporation of

Philadelphia, and in 1962 and 1964 the U.S. Navy flew additional magnetic profiles in the area. The implication of magnetic contours by Aero Services is that the crystalline or

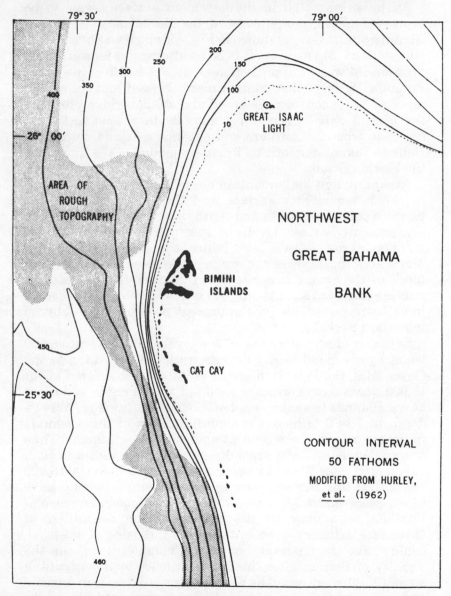

Figure A2—Bathymetry and rough bottom topography in the vicinity of the Bimini Islands.

sedimentary rock basement beneath the northwest Bahama Bank is generally deep, exhibits broad compositional changes, and is more continental than oceanic in crustal characteristics.

An important high in the basement surface seems to be expressed in the morphology of the Bank margin between Bimini and Cat Cay, as shown in Fig. A2 which was taken from Hurley, *et al.* (6) There seems to be no alternative reason for the pronounced westward projection (Figs. A1 & A2) of the Great Bahama Bank at this point. Indeed, Newell and Imbrie (7) reported ". . .a conspicuous broad and shallow ridge. . .termed the Bimini axis, which (axis) extends in a west-northwest direction from the northern end of Andros Island across the Bank to Bimini and forms a broad projection of the Bank into the Florida Straits."

Assuming that the "mountain peaks" could represent a high in the basement-rock surface and that they could lie just beneath portions of north and south Bimini, how is it that they are presently at sea level? Is this merely a result of the worldwide rise of sea level since the height of the last glaciation, 18,500 years ago, or has there been foundering of a block of the crust ("Poseidia") in this area, as suggested in reading number 12 of the original series? Or could both events have been responsible for the present position of the alleged mountain peaks?

Evidence of a relative rise of sea level at Bimini since 8,000 years ago is found in Kornicker's work. (8) According to the Cayce files, the Poseidian sector of Atlantis foundered about 10,000 years ago. Kornicker reported that a chain of former barrier islands lies submerged off South Cat Cay (Fig. A2) at a depth of 7 to 9 fathoms. The configuration of these islands indicates a former seastand at about minus 8 fathoms. Thus there is evidence for a seashore environment that has been submerged some 50 feet by rising sea level within the last 8,000 years. But this submergency by rising sea level would have taken place about 2,000 years after tectonic submergence of Poseidia, according to the readings. The deposition of carbonate sediment, concomitant with the rising of sea level, could have progressively covered "mountaintops" in the vicinity of Bimini, after their submergence by downfaulting some 10,000 years ago. The Florida Straits depression appears to be a fault depression, at least in the western part (9), and the possibility cannot be discounted that the Bahama Banks themselves could have been downfaulted at some prior point in time.

The author realized in 1962 that it would be necessary to penetrate the sediments and limestone crusts on Bimini in order to determine the nature of the rocks that composed the ground surface which has lain buried some 10,000 years. A preliminary reconnaissance in that year revealed that minor dredging near East Swell Inlet (also known as East Well or Muddy Creek Inlet) had not turned up anything significant in this part of the "north...portion...of the north island." Nor had any water wells, trenches, or canals been dug sufficiently deep, or in the right places, to permit encounter with the supposed pre-10,000-year-old rocks. In 1965, however, a channel was dredged for the Buccaneer Point Marina at the northern tip of South Bimini.

While inspecting carbonate sand and limestone dredge spoil (Fig. A1, "A") from the deepest part of the entrance channel, the author found a large pebble of serpentinite, completely encrusted with limestone. The specimen was submitted to an expert who examined a thin section of the fragment. The petrographer reported finding peridotite, chromite, bastite after hypersthene, kink-banding deformation in the pyroxene, and other features characteristic of serpentinized peridotites of the Alpine type.

The evidence argues strongly against the pebble being a piece of ship's ballast; it is possible, therefore, that it could be a pebble derived from an outcrop of serpentinite now buried more than 15 feet or so beneath limestone crusts and carbonate sediment. It could also have been transported into the area by prehistoric men who had access to the area by boat.

Also found at this site was a limestone-encrusted "coal" fragment. The fragment was examined thoroughly by a coal-petrographer of ten years' experience who reported that the fragment was of such high carbon content (98.3 percent) that it could only have come from either Pennsylvania, or some deposit of anthracite outside of North America. The fact that this piece of "coal" was in dredge spoil that originated about 12 feet below sea level, and several feet below the bottom, is merely noted in passing.

In addition to the fragments found at site A, the author was given a large piece of garnet-hornblende-granite gneiss by a native of North Bimini who said he had found it about three feet below the ground surface while digging a foundation trench for a circular sidewalk in front of the Avis-Bimini Hotel. (Fig. A3, "B") This piece may have been introduced somehow and its existence is again merely noted in passing.

In 1965, drill holes were put down at sites C (-27 ft.), D (-22 ft.), and E (-50 ft.). Megascopic examination of the cores and cuttings revealed carbonate rock and sand, exclusively. In 1966, borings (Fig. A1) were made at sites F (-40 ft.), G (-45 ft.), H (-40 ft.), and I (-45 ft.). Again, megascopic examination revealed carbonate material, exclusively. A study of the ratio of low-Mg calcite to aragonite in the core samples revealed the absence of aragonite in all borings below 26 feet below MLW. Thus, there is evidence that the Pleistocene-Recent boundary could be about 25 feet below tide along this line of cores and that the "mountain tops" could be composed of this carbonate rock.

Attention is turned to the nature of the "many various

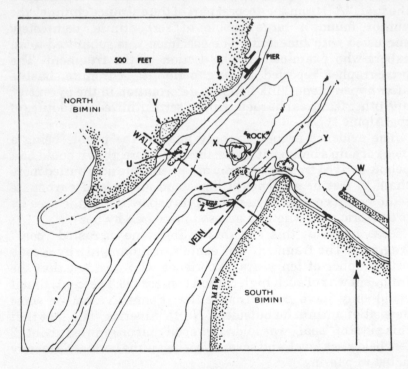

Figure A3—Bathymetry of the Bimini inlet, sample localities referred to in text, and possible location of the "wall" and "vein." Contours are in feet below mean high water (MHW).

minerals" that the readings mentioned could be found at Bimini, and to their location and depth in the ground. The answer to the question of vein minerals at Bimini is confusing because there are no known "icthyolite" minerals in the literature of mineralogy or petrology. Perhaps minerals associated with *ijolitic* rocks were meant. Interestingly, these rocks owe their characteristics largely to contamination of magma by assimilation of limestone, and may be found in serpentinized areas. Ijolites are characterized by a long list of accessory minerals such as apatite, sphene, calcite, melanite, phlogopite, sodalite, perovskite, wallastonite, cancrinite, pectolite, and zeolites, any of which may increase sufficiently in amount to become a major constituent. Some of the minerals just named are "spar" minerals.

The reference to "the walls as may be. . .builded" is, in the context of the entire reading, to a wall that would be built across the inlet at Entrance Point (Fig. A1), as a lock or dam for use in generating hydro-electric power. Using color aerial photographs, a map has been compiled (Fig. A3) showing the submarine topography in the inlet channel and the author's interpretation of the approximate position of the proposed wall, as well as the location of the vein.

Whether the "vein" would represent a linear deposit of gold and spar artifacts lying upon the carbonate rock of a buried "mountain top," or whether the gold and spar minerals would reside in a mineralized vein in a mountain top of igneous or metamorphic rock, are still subject to speculation. In any event, in 1967 the author found several fragments of a tough gray and brown slate on both sides of the inlet. (Fig. A3, sites "V" and "W") The carbonate materials in which these slate fragments were found were in both cases materials that had been removed from excavations at "U" and "Y" (Fig. A3), respectively.

In addition to the earlier borings elsewhere, three holes were drilled at sites "X", "Y", and "Z". (Fig. A3) Because of the light-weight rig that had to be used, it was impossible to penetrate to "the 12 to 15 foot levels" below the bottom. The hole at "X" penetrated 2.3 feet of either a limestone crust or material known as "beach rock." The presence of the pronounced circular rise on the bottom (Fig. A3, "Rock") at "X" is difficult to explain. It measures roughly 80 feet in diameter. Although it could be beach rock in its entirety it seems unlikely to find a mound of beach rock in the center of the main channel. Possibly the "rock" is a coral head covered with a veneer of beach rock.

The boring at "Y" penetrated only 4.8 feet of limestone crust before the drill stuck fast, because of the inadequate return of water up the casing. At "Z", an 8-foot thickness of sand was washed up the casing before drilling water was lost. One notes (Fig. A3) that the limestone bottom in this area of the inlet is covered with large underwater sand dunes which obscure the true nature of the hardrock surface.

Although the above investigations were inconclusive, they do provide a background of experience for future work. The author believes that the questions raised by his meager findings could be settled by drilling a line of holes, to about 40 feet below tide, along the line of the "wall" and the "vein." (Fig. A3) A high-volume water pump and a 4-in. diameter or larger drill would be needed to obtain usable cores in these honeycombed carbonate rocks.

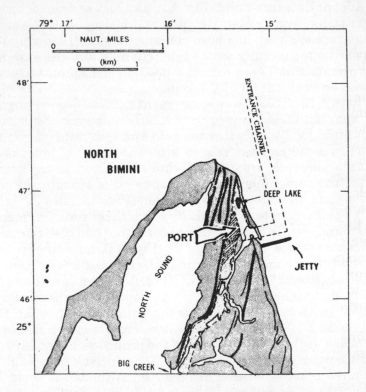

Figure A4—Map of region of suggested port development showing proposed entrance channel, jetty, and harbor area.

Figure A5—Silt-filled depression near Rocky Point, North Bimini, B.W.I.

The question of making Bimini into a shipping port by "opening of the channel" ["on the north end of the south portion of north island"] "to the west and to the north" makes good sense. The channel referred to is the tidal channel at East Swell Inlet (Fig. A1) and, as of the latter part of 1967, a large American corporation was contemplating a harbor development there using a quite similar approach. By dredging a channel in a westerly direction into the mangrove (Fig. A4) and then turning north, one would encounter the deep lake shown on Figures A1 and A4. The readings' recommendation for construction of a jetty (Fig. A4) on the south side of such an improved channel also makes sense because the net littoral drift in this region is from south to north. To an engineering geologist, this psychically obtained recommendation is a valid one.

A final comment is directed to "the well," which was located by reading 587-4 as being on the southeastern portion of the north island. The socialite aviatrix who requested this information actually went and found the well. The hole that she said she found (in 1935) was "a fresh-water well. . .walled around the top with stones of peculiar composition and strange symbols" (from correspondence on file at the Edgar Cayce Foundation). The author searched for this "well" and believes that the most likely candidate is a tidal pool located (Fig. A1) about 320 feet northwest of Rocky Point. The stones of peculiar composition were not seen, perhaps because hurricanes since 1936 have washed sand and silt into the depression. (Fig. A5) According to Gladys Davis Turner, an unrecorded reading for the aviatrix told her that the flow of the well was influenced by the tide.

Atlantean remains that are said to be beneath the eastern shore of north Bimini could be found only by extensive excavations in the beach rock along the coast. That anyone will go to the expense of such activity is questionable just now. It would be relatively inexpensive, however, to drill a 90-foot hole at D (Fig. A1) to the horizon where black sulphur water is alleged to be, and a thorough investigation of "the well" would be relatively easy and inexpensive to undertake.

Conclusions

Although valid clairvoyance is strongly in evidence in portions of the Edgar Cayce readings on the Bimini Islands, the definite field work required to prove or disprove the "Atlantean" statements remains to be accomplished. The precognitive accuracy of the records will be tested in 1968, inasmuch as one transcript states that in "sixty-eight and sixty-nine" there will be an emergence of the sea-floor near, or including, Bimini.

REFERENCES

1. S. Way, Paper 64 WA-ENER-7, Amer. Soc. Mech. Engineers, Ann. Meet., Nov. 1964; see also, *Mech. Eng.* 87, 142 (1965).
2. H.H. Hess, *Second Carib. Geol. Conf. Trans.,* Univ. Puerto Rico, 160 (1960).
3. N.D. Newell and J.K. Rigby, *Soc. Econ. Paleontol. and Mineral. Spec. Pub.,* 5, 15 (1957).
4. W. Harrison, *Geol. Soc. Amer. Abstr. Vol.* (1963)
5. R.E. Sheridan, *Masters Thesis,* Columbia Univ. (1965).
6. R.J. Hurley, *Bull. Marine Sci. Gulf and Carib.,* 12, 313 (1962).
7. N.D. Newell and J. Imbrie, *Trans. N.Y. Acad. Sci.* 3 (1955).
8. L.S. Kornicker, *Bull. Marine Sci. Gulf and Carib.,* 168 (1964).
9. J.W. Kofoed and R.J. Malloy, *Southeastern Geol.,* 6, 159 (1965).

About the Author

Hugh Lynn Cayce. For over 50 years Hugh Lynn Cayce guided and directed the work of making available to the public the psychic information of his father, Edgar Cayce. One of his greatest interests was in the area of earth changes and predictions; it was this interest that inspired *Earth Changes Update*. His other books include *Venture Inward, The Outer Limits of Edgar Cayce's Power,* and *Faces of Fear*.

A.R.E. PRESS

The A.R.E. Press publishes quality books, videos, and audio-tapes meant to improve the quality of our readers' lives—personally, professionally, and spiritually. We hope our products support your endeavors to realize your career potential, to enhance your relationships, to improve your health, and to encourage you to make the changes necessary to live a loving, joyful, and fulfilling life.

For more information or to receive a free catalog, call

> 1-800-723-1112

Or write

> A.R.E. Press
> P.O. Box 656
> Virginia Beach, VA 23451-0656